Why Trade It In?

Your Mechanic can save you money

GEORGE AND SUZANNE FREMON

Liberty Publishing Company

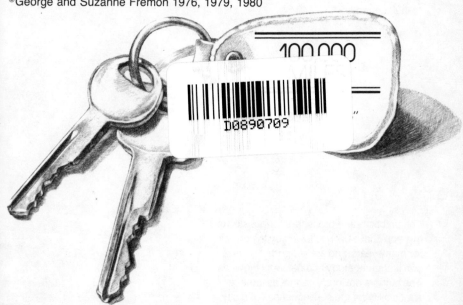

Published by:
Liberty Publishing Company
50 Scott Adam Road
Cockeysville, Maryland 21030

Library of Congress   76-42603
ISBN   0-89709-016-0

Manufactured USA

To ___ *ed:*

*t*___

and Reliable Old Bert,
this book is affectionately dedicated.

To the mechanics we have known and loved:

to Ashton,
and Joe,
and Andy,
and Frank,
and Leo,
and Angelo,
and Walt,
and Bill,
and Reliable Old Bert,

this book is affectionately dedicated.

CONTENTS

1. INTRODUCTION

This book is based on the concept that you can keep your car running *indefinitely* by practicing the same kind of preventive maintenance that takes you regularly to your doctor for a check-up and to your dentist for a cleaning and a going-over. As with your own physical condition, where you are trying to detect possible trouble before it compounds itself for lack of attention, or even becomes so serious as to shut you down, so with your automobile. You will not always be completely successful in either case, but with good management and moderately good luck, both you and your car can continue to operate in good condition, year after year after year.

A copy of this book, or one like it, should have been in the glove compartment of your automobile when it was driven away from the dealer by its first owner. "You have just spent $7,000 ($6,000? $8,000?) for this car," such a book should say, "which is the largest single purchase, except for a house, that most people ever make. It should serve you satisfactorily and safely for many years. This book will tell you how to derive full value for the money you have spent."

There was no such book in the glove compartment, nor was there anything like it available from the dealer or the manufacturer. The owner's manual that was in the glove compartment praised the manufacturer for having made such a magnificent artifact for your pleasure and convenience, told you how to start the engine, select the transmission settings, operate the power windows (optional), empty the ash trays, operate the cigarette lighter, fasten the safety harness, and remove ketchup and mustard stains from the upholstery. The technical information was often limited to what tire sizes to buy and what air pressure to put in them, what light bulbs to use for what applications, where to find most of the fuses (in many cases omitting any mention of the most important fuse), and what maintenance operations to have performed during the first 35,000 miles or so. Beyond that, silence. What the manufacturer doesn't tell you won't hurt him. Come back at 40,000 miles for further help, and he'll tell you that what you need is a brand-new car with a brand-new owner's manual in the glove compartment; it will cost you only your three-year-old car plus a few thousand dollars and change.

Many automobile owners don't like this answer. They would prefer to spend not several thousand dollars every three or four years but only a few hundred dollars over the same period, for a car they can trust. Many believe that a new car would not be better than the one they have now — that however tinny and junky the present one may be, the newer one would be even tinnier and junkier. And many of them wonder, too, whether it wouldn't be better for each of us individually and all of us together on our small planet to keep our present cars running smoothly for hundreds of thousands of miles, to keep each one in the family for as long as it can do its essential job, to develop a decent pride in saving money and preserving our resources, and finally to extricate ourselves from bondage to a single industry.

These are not trivial considerations. In 1978, one of the automobile industry's biggest years, the American people bought 11½ million new cars and "consumer" pickup trucks, and junked approximately 8½ million. (The automobile population is still rising slowly.) The average age of the cars that were hauled off to the junk yard was less than twelve years.

By any reasonable standards, those junk cars were too young to die. With only moderate expenditures for maintenance each year, the average age of cars thrown away can be twenty years instead of twelve; and to meet our national automobile requirements we would then have to manufacture and import only 7-9 million new cars instead of 10-12 million.

At 1978 prices, that saving — 3 to 4 million automobiles — represents about $24 billion worth of human effort, which could be going into other manufactures, facilities, and services. One of the services would indeed be maintenance of these automobiles for another year, and this would absorb about $2 billion of the $24 billion, leaving $22 billion potentially available for things other than automobiles.

A billion dollars is such a huge sum that it is meaningless; and $22 billion is twenty-two times as meaningless. But it may help in understanding it to reflect that the total salaries of all the public school teachers, principals, and supervisors in the United States in the year 1978 came to about $32 billion. So the human effort being wasted in producing more cars than we need — not the total spent on cars, mind you, but the effort *wasted* by building cars we don't need — has been more than two-thirds the total effort the country expends on public school teachers and administrators. Another measure: the U.S. Department of Agriculture had a budget in 1978 of $21.6 billion. Still others: in 1978 the budget of the Environmental Protection Agency was approximately one-fifth of the money wasted that year in manufacturing automobiles we didn't need; the National Science Foundation was roughly 4%; the Consumer

Product Safety Commission one-quarter of one percent.

The idea of increasing the average life of automobiles to 20 years is no idle dream. Between production line and junkyard, the average automobile is owned by three different people; if each of these owners were to maintain the car and keep it as long as it filled his needs and pleasures — say three years longer than he has been in the habit of doing — the life span of the average American car would automatically increase to at least 20 years and perhaps considerably longer.

For an individual automobile owner, this is an option that is open right this minute, beginning with whatever car he or she happens to own. It does not require a knowledge of engines or a talent for doing-it-yourself. It does require some degree of common sense and patience and confidence, all of which can be developed. Ordinary help from service stations, garages, and body shops will do the rest. And the car will go on and on and on, year after year, providing reliable transportation, as long as the owner wishes.

The purpose of this book is to describe in considerable detail how to do this.

2. WHAT THIS BOOK IS ABOUT

This book does not tell you *how* to repair or adjust or inspect or replace *anything*. It is intended for that segment of our technological culture that is without wrenches, screwdrivers, mechanical judgment, or grease under the fingernails, and also without the wish to acquire any of these.

It is intended to help these people keep their cars running indefinitely without having to do the work themselves.

To reach this end, you will need the services of a conscientious, moderately-competent mechanic. Finding such a person will not be the easiest job you ever undertook, but neither is it impossible. On page 55 begins a section called "Your Mechanic and You," in which you may find some helpful suggestions.

You will then tell the mechanic what you want him to do, and when. To guide you in this endeavor, the Maintenance Schedule, beginning on page 71, is organized according to the mileage reading on your odometer. The Maintenance Schedule is the most important part of this book. It is your primary tool for keeping your car in satisfactory service for 200,000 miles, or 300,000 if you wish.

You will find in this schedule instructions to replace various parts of your automobile before they are worn out. This may shock you — it is certain to cause some discussion with your mechanic — but upon reflection you will recognize that it is preferable to remove an aging fuel pump, for example, and replace it with a new one *before,* not *after,* it shuts you down.

The other major tool offered here is the list of Symptoms, beginning on page 95. This list recites many of the sounds, the shudders, the stinks, and the unwelcome silences that all cars, however well maintained, are vulnerable to at any age beyond the cradle. In this list we suggest what might be wrong, and how urgent it is to do something about it.

"But Repairs Are Such A Hassle!" is a discussion, beginning on page 45, dedicated to all fellow sufferers, in the recognition that in the area of car ownership, unless you take charge you can't win. A car that continually breaks down is a pain; a new car that is riddled with new-car complaints is also a pain. The answer is to avoid the breakdowns by taking action ahead of time. It's the only way you can win.

You may also want to keep your car looking respectable. Not everyone cares about this, but many people do; if you are among them, there is a section for you, beginning on page 63, where you will find an introduction to body shops.

If you have a record-keeping mentality, you may be interested in the recommendation, beginning on page 52, that you keep a notebook in your car.

Near the end of the book, just before the Index, there is a glossary — definitions of a few automotive terms that didn't fit easily into the text. If the word you want is not there, try a dictionary.

As for why bother? the following three chapters offer some reasons for keeping your present car and maintaining it properly, instead of buying a new one.

The reasons are these: it's cheaper, it's more sensible, and it's less wasteful. If you already know all that, and are familiar with the facts and figures on which those reasons are based, you don't need to read these chapters. But we had to write them.

The rest of the book, a large section called "Your Car" and devoted to descriptions of the workings of the automobile, with illustrations, is included to provide information for several additional levels of interest. When you say to your mechanic, "Please re-gap the spark plugs," which you will say to him every 10,000 miles, as directed on page 80, you don't have to know what you're talking about. The mechanic will understand the words even if you don't. But if you want to know what you're asking, or if you have some stirrings of curiosity about spark plugs, you can find a general statement about them and their function by following the page reference at the spark-plug item in the Maintenance Schedule. This will take you to page 183, where they are explained.

If your curiosity is somewhat greater and if you want to know how spark plugs fit into the larger scheme of things, you can browse among the items leading up to and following the description of spark plugs, even perhaps going so far as to read the whole section on the ignition system, starting on page 178.

An automobile is an ingenious and complex machine, made up of hundreds of parts organized into systems (fuel system, brake system, charging system, etc.) which in turn are neatly interrelated. But this need not overwhelm you: the parts individually are simple, and an engine and its support systems are not difficult to understand if you take it piece by piece and recognize that there's no hurry — you have the rest of your life. And it's a pleasurable intellectual exercise; it stretches the mind a bit.

In addition, understanding an automobile gives its owner a much-needed sense of adequacy: it is possible, after all, for a human being to be the equal of a machine.

3. ONE GOOD REASON FOR KEEPING YOUR PRESENT CAR: IT'S CHEAPER

If you bought a new car, you would spend more money right now than you would spend to keep your present car in superb condition for 10 years.

You may not be able to take this proposition seriously at first. All our lives we have been hearing that the wise thing to do with your car is to trade it in while its trade-in value is still substantial and before repair bills begin to eat you up. Some people believe two years is the optimum period to keep a car; others believe in a three-year cycle; others say four, and still others opt for five as the magic number. But however much the individual believers may disagree on details — and however much they may resent the necessity for their beliefs — they are in solid agreement on one main point: the time will come, fairly soon, when they will spend more money on repairs than they would spend on a new car.

This is not true. It is a myth, the oldest and most pervasive of all the Great Automobile Myths.

It is impossible to spend as much money keeping a car in tip-top condition for years to come as you would lose in depreciation on a new car.

And the longer you keep your present car, the more money you will save.

Another related myth has come into being as the price of gasoline has increased in recent years. This newer myth says that you will save money in the long run if you get rid of your big old gas-guzzler and buy a new high-mileage small car; you could soon pay for the new car out of your gasoline savings.

This proposition is no more true than the first one. Gasoline savings would not be likely to exceed what you spend on the swap in under 125,000 miles, and it is entirely possible that the break-even point would not be reached in under 250,000 miles. And furthermore, to throw away an operating automobile and subsidize the manufacture of another one that is not needed is to indulge in a degree of wastefulness that we simply cannot afford, either as individuals or as inhabitants of a world with limited resources.

It is obviously not enough simply to make these assertions. They must be backed up with figures. The remainder of this chapter will be devoted to figures and to the hope of putting to rest for all time the preposterous notion that a $300 garage bill is somehow more expensive than a $6,000 or $8,000 new car.

The two myths can be examined together by means of a simple example in which two sets of figures are compared: the probable cost over a five-year period if you keep your present car well maintained, and the probable cost over the same period if you buy a new car. The figures are set out in table form on page 14. Your own situation may differ somewhat from these figures — they are drawn from national averages — and you may want to make corrections to the table. Whatever figures you use will tell you the same story.

The examples are based on the following assumptions:

1. All of the cited dollar amounts are subject to further inflation (or to deflation, if it should occur), but the costs will rise and fall more or less together as the

Notes on these assumptions

A. Automobile prices are changing so rapidly that any specific number used for illustration will almost certainly appear quaint within a few months. These estimates are based on a wide array of automobile-industry and government publications, updated on the basis of recent newspaper and magazine reports. Unfortunately, the only way to find out how much it would cost to replace your present car with a new one is to have a serious talk with an automobile dealer. Don't assume that a price picture you established three or four months ago is still applicable.

B. Current automobile advertisements about the mileages you can expect from new cars are not to be trusted. Before you judge the figures in the table, please read "A Special Note About Gasoline Mileage" on page 18.

C. The estimates of maintenance costs are based upon a wide variety of published sources and also on our own experience, the experiences of friends whose reports and records we trust, and extensive conversations with garage operators. One extreme case is our 1962 Cadillac, which we bought in 1970 for $375, knowing that it was in particularly run-down condition. Over the ensuing five years, repairs and rehabilitation cost $900 immediately and then $675 per year. At the other extreme is our 1964 Falcon, bought at age 10 at a cost of $650, *including* the cost of overdue repairs that had to be done immediately. Over the ensuing *two years* it required $250 for maintenance. Two 1966 Fords fall in between: a Fairlane that cost $885 for maintenance during its eighth, ninth, and tenth years (for an avareage of $292 per year), and a Galaxie that cost $1200 ($400 per year) during the same period.

dollar changes in value, and the relationships will not change appreciably. All prices and costs, past, present, and future, are expressed in current dollars.

2. If your present car is old enough to cause you to think about a new car, its trade-in value will cover only a small part of the cost of the new car you would select as a replacement. The more valuable the car you own at the time you decide to buy a new one, the more expensive will be the minimum new car you would accept as a replacement. You would spend $5,000 to $7,000 plus your present car for a new one; in the example the assumption is that you would spend $6,000.

3. You would have to pay sales tax at 5 percent on the $6,000 net difference: $300. Also, you would probably borrow the $6,300 you need, at a finance charge of about $350 per thousand dollars borrowed ($2,200). The entire $8,500 would be paid off in 60 monthly installments of $142.

4. In deference to the gloomy energy outlook and to your own pocketbook you would probably select a smaller car than your present one. At whatever cost in comfort, the new car would achieve 25 miles per gallon instead of the 12 you suffer now. You drive the car about 12,000 miles per year, and gasoline costs about $1.20 per gallon. The present car requires 1,000 gallons of gasoline ($1,200) for 12,000 miles, and the new one would require 480 gallons ($576), so the saving would be $624 per year.

5. You would carry substantially more insurance on the new car — at minimum, $175 more in premium the first year, and $150, $125, $100, and $75 the second, third, fourth, and fifth years, respectively.

6. If all went well, you would incur no substantial expenses not covered by warranty during the first two years, but during the third, fourth, and fifth years, maintenance costs (as opposed to operating expenses) would be $275, $350, and $475, respectively.

7. If you are on the brink of buying a new car, you have probably been skimping on maintenance for the

past year or two; so it is sensible to assume that you would spend $600 or even $900 for maintenance during the first year you decide to *not* buy a new car. In subsequent years, complete maintenance would average out, at worst, in the neighborhood of $500 to $700 per year. The word "average" is important: in a good year, maintenance costs may be as low as a hundred or two hundred dollars, only to jump up to seven or eight hundred in a later year and then subside again.

8. In order to compare two courses of action fairly it is essential to take credit for interest on money you do *not* spend. If you elect to pay a finance company $142 a month, you must take that money away from the rest of your life in order to hand it over. For purposes of comparison, the alternative to paying it over to the finance company is to pay it over to a bank, for deposit in a savings account. As this is written, ordinary savings accounts pay interest ranging from 5 percent compounded quarterly to 5½ percent compounded daily; in the example we assume 5½ percent compounded monthly.

The economics of buying a new car are compared with the economics of not buying a new car in the table on page 14. In the first column are expenditures that would have to be made for monthly payments, gasoline (at 25 miles per gallon), and repairs (as opposed to operating expenses) if you bought a new car. In the second column we show estimates of expenditures for gasoline (at 12 miles per gallon) and repairs required to keep your present car in superb condition, based upon the assumptions described in the preceding paragraphs. Please note that the table lists only the items of automobile expense that would not be the same for your present car and a hypothetical new car. Gasoline expenditures are included, for example, but not expenditures for tires, batteries, lubrication, tune-ups, and other things and services that a newer automobile would require too. Interest is included for the reasons set forth in paragraph 8, above. It is a sizable item in the accounts, and it particularly deserves mention because it is so often ignored by the watchdog of a family's finances. Understandably, this faithful guardian is usually preoccupied with the basic question, "Can we make the monthly payments?" The *cost* of making those payments is seldom given much thought, because most people don't realize that they have a choice in the matter: they "need" a new car; it costs a substantial amount of money ($2,200, based on the assumptions of page 11) to borrow the money to pay for that car; they simply add that charge to the cost of the car and try to forget about it. But, as they will discover if they decline to buy a new car, they will not only save the interest on the money they are not borrowing, they will actually draw interest themselves on that money. For once in their lives they will be on the right side.

This fact will come through best for you if you recognize that by not spending money on a new car you are going to have money to use for something else. The obvious thing to do as a starter is to open a new savings account — the No-New-Car-Now account, perhaps? — and feed into it every month the money you would otherwise be paying over to the finance company. Out of the account would have to come the money to pay for repairs to your present car and a monthly allowance to cover whatever difference there is in the gasoline appetites of the two cars. What is left in the new savings account will grow and grow and grow. According to our experience, after five years your balance will be of the order of $4,000 to $5,000, and it is more likely to be higher than lower. At some point along the way, you will have a difficult decision to make: how much should you let it grow? You may consider the possibility of buying a new car, or at any rate a newer car, but by then you may have concluded that Old Faithful has served so well all these years, it might as well do a few more, and you would rather spend the money on a trip to Europe. And if you do decide to buy another car with your accumulated savings, you will at least be able to buy it for cash and save yourself another set of interest payments.

MAKING MONEY BY *NOT* BUYING A NEW CAR
How Your Bank Account Can Grow

Even assuming a rising trend in the prices of gasoline and maintenance, which now seems likely, you will still enjoy considerable savings by deferring the purchase of a new car.

FIRST YEAR

Deposit the amounts you would have spent on the new car you didn't buy:

12 monthly payments of $142	$1,704
Additional insurance premium	175
Gasoline: 480 gallons @ $1.20	576
Maintenance	125
Total deposits.	2,580

Withdraw amounts to pay expenses of the car you did not trade in:

Gasoline: 1,000 gallons @ $1.20	1,200
Rehabilitation and maintenance in first year	750
Total withdrawals.	1,950
Deposits minus withdrawals	630
Interest on the account, first year	19
Balance in account, end of first year	$ 649

SECOND YEAR

Deposit the amounts you would have spent on the new car you didn't buy:

12 monthly payments of $142	$1,704
Additional insurance premium	150
Gasoline: 480 gallons @ $1.20.	576
Maintenance	150
Total deposits.	2,580

Withdraw amounts to pay expenses of the car you did not trade in:

Gasoline: 1,000 gallons @ $1.20	1,200
Maintenance:	600
Total withdrawals.	1,800
Deposits minus withdrawals	780
Interest on the account, second year	61
Balance in account, end of second year	$1,490

THIRD YEAR

Deposit the amounts you would have spent on the new car you didn't buy:

12 monthly payments of $142	$1,704
Additional insurance premium	125
Gasoline: 480 gallons @ $1.20	576
Maintenance	275
Total deposits	2,680

Withdraw amounts to pay expenses of the car you did not trade in:

Gasoline: 1,000 gallons @ $1.20	1,200
Maintenance:	600
Total withdrawals	1,800
Deposits minus withdrawals	880
Interest on the account, third year	111
Balance in account, end of third year	$2,481

FOURTH YEAR

Deposit the amounts you would have spent on the new car you didn't buy:

12 monthly payments of $142	$1,704
Additional insurance premium	100
Gasoline: 480 gallons @ $1.20	576
Maintenance	350
Total deposits	2,730

Withdraw amounts to pay expenses of the car you did not trade in:

Gasoline: 1,000 gallons @ $1.20	1,200
Maintenance:	600
Total withdrawals	1,800
Deposits minus withdrawals	930
Interest on the account, fourth year	169
Balance in account, end of fourth year	$3,580

FIFTH YEAR

Deposit the amounts you would have spent on the new car you didn't buy:

12 monthly payments of $142	$1,704
Additional insurance premium	75
Gasoline: 480 gallons @ $1.20	576
Maintenance	475
Total deposits	2,830

Withdraw amounts to pay expenses of the car you did not trade in:

Gasoline: 1,000 gallons @ $1.20	1,200
Maintenance:	600
Total withdrawals	1,800
Deposits minus withdrawals	1,030
Interest on the account, fifth year	233
Balance in account, end of fifth year	$4,843

Another consideration may occur to you as you ponder this question of finances, and you might express it this way: "If I keep my present car, which is five years old, for another five years, it will be ten years old, and practically worthless. If I get a new car now and keep it for five years, it will only be five years old, and worth at least something." What you are thinking about here is the trade-in values of the two cars, and the depreciation rate of cars in general, and it may seem reasonable to take all that into account when you are trying to decide which course of action is more economical. After all, you may argue to yourself, the value of my car five years from now has a bearing on the subject.

It does indeed have a bearing if you are certain you will sell it; the "worth" of a car, according to automobile dealers, is what they are prepared to allow you for it on the purchase of another car. And if you are going to buy another car, that allowance should figure into the deal.

On the other hand, the difference in dollars between the allowance on a five-year-old car and a ten-year-old car is relatively small. By the mysterious laws that govern this matter, a car loses one-fourth to one-third of its value every year from the day it is sold. The first year, that loss is, say, 30 percent of its purchase price; the second year, 30 percent of its one-year-old value; the third year, 30 percent of its two-year-old value; and so on. This means that by the time a car is five years old, 30 percent of its value is a much smaller number of dollars than that same fraction was a couple of years before. And the ensuing years take off smaller and smaller numbers of dollars. So your loss in dollars is cut down with every passing year.

The commercial world of the automobile is dominated by the "book value" of used cars. This means what a car would bring at auction. But book value has meaning only if you are selling a car. If, five years from now, your present car is eight years old, or ten, or twelve, and it is still running as though it will last as long as you do, it isn't going to matter to you whether its

book value is $237.00 or $23.70. Its true value to you
will be expressible in quite different terms.

    The comparison on page 14 between present-car
economics and new-car economics has been deliberately weighted toward the new-car side, in an effort not
to over-sell.
    It is unlikely, for example, that your present car will
require $600 per year in maintenance ($50 deposited in
the bank every month), and it is unlikely that you would
actually gain gasoline mileage of 13 miles per gallon by buying a new car. Also, it is valid to question
whether you would cling for five years to a new car you
would buy today, because the chances of selecting one
that will really please you,or that will be free of hassle, or
that will serve your needs, are slimmer than they used to
be. But even so weighted, and taking into account all the
relevant factors, the arithmetic adds up to the same conclusion: it is *not* cheaper to buy a new car than to keep
your present car and maintain it in superb condition.

    There are many good reasons for buying a new car.
Some people love new cars, as other people love food,
or drink, or friends, or family. They would rather have a
new car than a tour of the Rockies or a month in Lon-
don; they revel in the new-car smell, and they actively
enjoy washing and polishing the shiny exterior and
sweeping the carpets and emptying the ashtrays. Other
people actually need a car that is different from their
present one: larger, to take care of more or larger chil-
dren or animals or both; or smaller, now that the chil-
dren have grown up and gone; or more rugged, now
that the family has forsaken the suburbs for a farm. Still
others would genuinely prefer to take their chances with
a new car, however expensive and however uncertain,
than to think about maintenance problems at all. These
are all sensible and defensible reasons for buying a new
car.

The reason that is not sensible, and not defensible, is that a car has arrived at an age when it is "time to trade it in." There is no such time, and to believe that there is such a time is to be a victim of the Great Automobile Myth.

A SPECIAL NOTE ABOUT GASOLINE MILEAGE:

One of the major assumptions in the analysis of your present car versus a new car is that a new car would give you 25 miles per gallon of gasoline whereas your present car gives you only 12 MPG. Over a period of five years, an improvement of 13 MPG in your gasoline mileage would save you (counting interest) almost $3,500 if you drive 12,000 miles a year and if gasoline cost $1.20 a gallon. This is worth considering.

But if an important reason for thinking about a new car is to achieve better gasoline mileage, be sure that new car would actually achieve better gasoline mileage. *This is a warning.* Car advertisements are not to be trusted in this regard. One says: "20 MPG in the city and 27 MPG on the highway, according to EPA results.*" The asterisk refers you to a footnote, in much smaller type: "Mileage figures estimated are sales weighted averages. Actual mileage achieved will depend on where and how you drive, condition of the car, and optional equipment selected." If you were born earlier than yesterday, you will recognize this footnote as the manufacturer's warning that *you* will not be able to achieve 20 to 27 MPG. An automobile expert quoted in *The New York Times* a few years ago said, "There is no way in the world that you or I or anybody can obtain the mileages indicated by the tests." In another *New York*

Times article shortly thereafter, two drivers of the high-mileage Volkswagen Rabbit, touted in ads as getting 38 MPG according to EPA tests, compared their experiences. " 'I put 500 miles on one and a good part of it was on freeways, and all I got was 24.5,' complained one. 'That's just what I got,' replied the second.'' The actual mileages achieved by these two drivers were less than two-thirds of the advertised promise. So if either of these drivers had bought a VW Rabbit as a money-saving measure, basing their calculations on 38 MPG, they would have come to the end of a five-year period of 12,000 miles per year, having spent approximately 55% more for gasoline than they had figured on.

There is no evidence at the time of this writing that the Environmental Protection Agency (EPA) of the U.S. government has deliberately set up a mileage test for the purpose of defrauding the public. But any automobile owner who takes these test results seriously will *feel* defrauded, and with good reason. The EPA tests are run on a "dynamometer", which is a piece of laboratory equipment. The tests are not run on a road at all, or even on a test track. The laboratory-machine measurements are translated into "miles per gallon" by means of formulas based on numerous factors such as automobile weight, gear ratios, auxiliary equipment, and so on. The EPA has protected itself by publishing its procedures and standards, and the automobile manufacturers have protected themselves with their small-type footnotes; so if you come around complaining about institutionalized fraud you won't have a leg to stand on. You will have defrauded yourself by believing what you read in the advertisements.

What *can* you believe?

It is probably safe to believe that you will achieve about 75% of the gasoline mileages promised by the EPA tests. This conclusion is tentative, but it is based on extensive reading of newspaper and magazine reports and on a number of personal reports. There's nothing scientific about the conclusion, but on the whole it is sensible. So when you are looking for a new car that will give you 25 MPG, as compared with your present car, which gives only 12, you should be thinking about cars that advertise "EPA estimate" mileage ratings of 33 MPG at the very least. You could probably achieve such mileages in some minicompact and subcompact cars with manual transmission and no air-conditioning or other frills.

As gasoline prices climb and climb, you may well be thinking: "A new small car would soon pay for itself out of what we would save in fuel." This is an attractive idea, and widely held. Unfortunately, it is wrong if your driving mileage is typical.

Using the assumptions on which the table on pages 14-15 is based, and carrying out the calculations beyond five years, the following facts emerge:

1. If you bought a car that really did average 25 MPG, you would break even in *15 years;*

2. If you wanted to bring your break-even point down to 10 years from the date of purchase, you would have to find a car that averaged *40 MPG*, year in, year out; and

3. If your new car actually averaged only 20 MPG, you wouldn't break even in less than *24 years!*

4. THE VILLAIN OF THE PIECE: THE ANNUAL MODEL

In trying to understand the popular attitude toward automobiles, it is instructive to ponder the self-deception we indulge in when we tell ourselves that we'll save money in the long run if we turn in the old car on a new one every three or four or five years. Why in the world do we do it?

We don't fool ourselves in this way when we buy other things. Refrigerators, for example. As householders we buy new refrigerators because the old one has finally quit, or because it is too small for the growing family, or because it doesn't have enough freezer space, or because for the first time we have enough money to get a really decent one: all sensible reasons. A refrigerator is an outright purchase and we are aware that we are spending a certain amount of money to buy something we want or need. We don't tell ourselves and our friends and family any absurdity about how we're beating the game when we turn in the old refrigerator on a new one.

But at the same time that we are being sensible about the new refrigerator we are demonstrating an interesting lack of common sense about our automobiles.

At the bottom of the nonsense about automobiles is the concept of exorbitant depreciation. This word — depreciation — is one we all know and use and accept, but most of us have never examined what it is we are talking about it. We never doubt the "law" that an automobile loses value, beginning the instant it is driven out of the dealer's showroom, to the extent of almost 30% every year, with little regard for its condition, or how far it has been driven, or whether the tires are new or threadbare, or its value as transportation. For example: a car that you bought three years ago for $7,000 was "worth" $5,050 one year later (see the note on inflation on page 9); at age two it lost almost 30% of that figure and was worth $3,600; by now, at age three, it has lost 30% of its two-year value and is worth $2,525. Next year it will be worth $1,725; the following year $1,125. By the time it is 10 years old, the depreciation will have taken care of the value of the car. It will be worth very little. What a dealer will give you for it as trade-in on a new car will depend primarily on how much the dealer wants to reduce his price on the new automobile in order to close the deal.

And yet a 10-year-old car is still an operating vehicle, and if it has been taken care of it will be capable of going everywhere a new car can go, it will go as fast and as smoothly as a new car, and it will be as reliable and as safe. In fact, it may even be safer, since not all new cars are entirely safe, as witness the call-backs in recent years for faulty parts and faulty design. If its appearance has also been taken care of, a 10-year-old car can even look as good as a new car. And yet this car, in superb condition, is valued at next-to-nothing, while a new car is "worth" $6,000, or $7,000, or $8,000.

How ludicrous this proposition would be if it were applied to houses! Imagine: you go to a real estate agent to turn in your house on a new model. You bought the house three years ago for $60,000. The agent inspects your house in a cursory manner to find out what condition it is in, whether the furnace works, or the roof leaks, or what the paint looks like, or whether your children have wrecked the playroom. He consults a small book and tells you that your house is worth $21,700 as trade-in on a new $60,000 house. You protest that you have taken good care of it, that everything works fine, the paint looks new — in fact, some of it is new — you put in $300 worth of shrubbery two years ago, and the playroom has been used only on Sundays by your elderly aunt. Yes of course, the agent says, it's obviously in good condition — that's why he will allow you the $21,700 figure, from the "good condition" column; but what the hell, the agent likes you, and would like you to live in this new house; so he'll allow you $24,000.

Applied to houses, this practice would be madness. Houses, we know, tend to increase in value with age, and some of the country's most valuable houses are among the oldest. Part of the reason for this has to do with the state of the housing industry, part with inflation, but part is also that people take care of their houses. People expect their houses to last; they maintain them carefully — often lovingly — and they improve them if they can afford to. They fully expect that when the time comes to sell a house, it will be worth more, not less, than it was when they bought it.

This is not to say that automobiles and houses are entirely comparable, but it is to draw attention to the fact that our attitudes toward the aging of automobiles are the result of a major selling job. The manufacturers of automobiles have put over on us one of the cleverest merchandising ideas in industrial history: The Annual Model.

The Annual Model was invented in 1923 by a team in the General Motors organization who have come to be regarded as heroes of the automobile industry: Alfred Sloan, William Knudsen, and Charles Kettering. General Motors at that time had been unable to compete successfully with the Model T Ford, and the company was in trouble. The Model T had been on the market for 15 years; improvements had been added as they were developed, but there had been no revolutionary change in the basic design. There was no such thing as a 1921-model Ford; it looked from the outside much like its immediate predecessors and successors.

This fact gave the General Motors team the opening it needed for its sales gimmick — the Annual Model. The 1925 Chevrolet was a New Model, it was trumpeted. So was the 1926 Chevrolet. And so was the 1927 Chevrolet. The gimmick worked: the Model T was out of business within three years, and all the automobile manufacturers thereafter adopted the practice of the new model every year.

In the early days of the automobile, genuine innovations and improvements came in rapid succession, and obsolescence was swift and sure. The automobile with acetylene headlights, for example, was entirely outclassed by the one that mounted electric lights; the electric starter rendered obsolete — and rightly — all the cars that had to be cranked by hand. Less spectacular but also profoundly important were improvements in brakes, wheels and rims, transmissions, whole engine designs, and materials of construction from stem to stern. At this stage in the development of automobiles, owners had good reasons to replace their old cars with new ones as often as they could afford to, because the new ones were unquestionably safer, more comfortable, more convenient, and more reliable.

By 1925, however, major improvements had become much less frequent and much less major than they had been only a few years earlier, and as the years passed they became less frequent and less major still. Thus the Annual Model served a second function: introduced mainly as part of the desperate effort to unseat the Model T Ford, before long it became a device for avoiding a nightmare that haunted the industry — the coming of a time when the automobile owner would buy a car and keep it for as long as it served his transportation needs adequately. This was a gloomy prospect indeed for the automobile manufacturers, who were not in the business of serving the transportation needs of the public, but in the business of manufacturing and selling automobiles, and the more the better. Thus did the industry get into show business.

In the absence of real improvements, the Annual Model introduced yearly changes that were predominantly and in some years exclusively either cosmetic or gimmicky: the shape of the windows, the line of the fenders, the interior decor, the length and breadth and height, the color. Recently, for instance, we have had square headlight bulbs, which are no better functionally than their predecessors and cost over twice as much, and disappearing windshield-wiper blades, which get snowed in so solidly in their retracted position that a major excavating job is required to free them so they will wipe the windshield. These changes are like the periodic changes in fashions in clothing, and they are introduced for the same purpose: to cause us to become dissatisfied with what we have, and to buy replacements.

The annual Automobile Show was an early device for pushing the "new" cars, and it serves to demonstrate the industry's close connection with show business: it was and is today a theatrical production. Newspapers, always eager for advertising, instituted and still carry special supplements in which the ads are separated by earnest discussions of the "new" features written by people called "auto reporters" or "auto editors."

With the coming of television and huge new audiences hitherto untouched, the stage on which the Annual Model could be shown and touted expanded to include all possible terrains and all possible circumstances. The advertising of automobiles then became Big Business, too, with a huge stake in the continuation — and expansion — of the auto manufacturing industry.

We all know how automobiles are advertised: we are bombarded every day with sales pitches. Some in the audience recognize the pitches for what they are: efforts to persuade people to buy something they don't

need. But even many of these people are not sophisticated enough mechanically to judge whether a particular change has some real importance or is only a salesman spinning his web. Some of us tend to believe what
we are told, if only the tone of voice used in the telling is
authoritative enough. And all of us, it must be admitted,
are likely to be susceptible to one or another of the
salesmen's appeals.

The most obvious, of course, are related to sex and
power: the gorgeous female who caresses the new car,
and by implication, one supposes, the owner of the new
car; the he-man, dressed in appropriate he-man-type
clothes, punishing his car at will. He careens across
empty desert landscapes — traffic, incidentally, is never
a problem in automobile commercials — or he bounces
up dry creek beds, or hurtles off the top of rocky hills and
down into gullies. And these commercials, let us remember, are aimed at us, the people whose primary use
for our cars is to drive to the supermarket, back and
forth to work, and along the freeway to see grandma.

Now and then a series of ads based on normal — or
fairly normal — life comes along. We see just-plain-
folks, washing their cars in their driveways, or taking the
kids to Scout meetings. These people customarily respond to a neighbor's new car with an astonished
"Wow!" as though they had never seen an automobile
before in their lives.

The names automobiles are given are another aspect of the selling. They are clearly meant to appeal to
buried yearnings in human beings caught up unwillingly
in civilization. Part of their appeal, too, is in their am-
biguity. "Matador," for example, evokes visions of
courage and glamor in distant romantic lands; the word
also literally means "killer." "Cougar" and "Barracuda"
mean swiftness and strength; they, too, are killers and
wild and free in the bargain. Other names are more
direct in their appeal: "Grand Prix" and "Le Mans" are
clearly designed to persuade you that your mass-
produced Pontiac in which you drive to the movies

somehow shares the field with the other racers on the European tracks. And the smaller, less murderous animals — Impala, Pinto, Mustang — are graceful, or cute, or energetic, or endearing, and they all bring an exotic touch to our ordinary lives. The place names, oddly, appear to be mostly from the Caribbean or the Mediterranean or the Spanish-speaking parts of our own country — Granada, Eldorado, Seville, Capri, Catalina, Montego, Ventura, Cordoba, Riviera, Monte Carlo — suggesting hot, bright places to appeal to people whose lives are presumed to be cold and gray.

The cost of all this nonsense is enormous, of course. In 1974, the four largest advertisers among the automobile companies — General Motors, Ford, Chrysler, and Volkswagen of America — spent $509,600,000 on advertising. That's half-a-billion dollars plus nearly ten million more — added to the prices · of the cars sold by these companies, and paid for by those of us who bought them!

Whatever we may think of the ads and television commercials we are paying for, from the point of view of the automobile industry, the result has been unprecedented success and enormous power. The hundreds of millions of dollars spent on advertising every year has been worth every penny. The manufacturing of cars has grown from just another business to the single most important economic force in the nation. Economists have estimated that 25% of our national economic effort has come to be connected directly or indirectly with the automobile and much of this growth is a result of the generation-long barrage of expert selling techniques.

We can't blame it all on other people, however, even on the voracious auto manufacturers and their clever ad men. They couldn't have sold us so completely if we hadn't wanted to be sold. The fact is that we have cooperated willingly — even eagerly — in our own manipulation. Although we started out, in the early days of the automobile, as a nation of mechanics able to understand and even repair our own cars, we have long since abdicated this role and are no longer even able to judge the quality of the repair jobs we pay so highly for. Automobiles have become toys — the most expensive toys any civilization ever produced, surely, unless you count armaments as toys — and status symbols, and measures of value and taste, and the single most pervasive subject of conversation in almost any gathering of Americans. We are so hooked on cars that even when we are hard up, when the country as a whole is in a recession, when unemployment climbs and money is scarce and expensive, the automobile industry is able to *raise* the prices of cars, and people go on buying them.

Perhaps the most important consequence of our eager subjection to the automobile industry is our cheerful scuttling of all other means of transportation. There was a time when it was possible, and in fact customary, to walk to the grocery store, to ride the street car to work, to take the train for longer trips. Now, after 50 years of supporting automobiles and discouraging all other forms of transportation, our trains are bankrupt, street cars have vanished, and acres of new communities are built every year with not a sidewalk in sight. The process has been circular: the automobile has made sprawling possible and endurable; therefore we sprawl. Since we no longer need to walk to market, we build neighborhoods in which it is impossible to walk to market. The result of all this is that except for the residents of a few cities, each of us must have a car simply to get around on our daily business and pleasure.

This situation contributes to the myth that a new car is automatically better than an older car. When you *must* have a car, then it is urgent to have a trouble-free car; and if you persist in believing, in spite of evidence to the contrary, that only a new car can be free of trouble, the result is inevitably a leaning toward buying a new car if you can possibly afford it, and yet another solemn explanation to family and friends that you can't afford *not* to buy a new car.

If we want to get the automobile manufacturers off

our backs we must first of all learn the arithmetic of buying and operating automobiles and develop the courage to use it. We must also develop a healthy respect for compound interest, whether we understand the arithmetic of it or not, remembering that compound interest is with us every day of our lives, working either for us or against us — and develop the determination to be on the *income* side of compound interest, not the *paying* side. We must realize that automobile depreciation figures so unthinkingly bandied about are for the sheep, and that the value of a car to the owner is not what some little book says it is worth, but how much it would cost the owner to replace it. And perhaps most important of all, we must learn to distinguish for ourselves, with whatever help we may be able to get from our mechanic friend, Reliable Old Bert, between a genuine technological improvement and a breakthrough in salesmen's ballyhoo. We must recognize the Annual Model for the institutionalized fraud it was in the beginning, is now, and ever shall be unless the sheep start doing their own thinking.

Not all changes in automobiles are entirely cosmetic. Over the past 30 or 40 years there have been several real improvements. Materials and engineering skills have advanced steadily, and there have been a few major technical advances: hydraulic brakes in the late thirties; sealed-beam headlights about 1940; automatic transmissions in the late thirties; power brakes, power steering, and air-conditioning in the early to middle fifties; the dual brake system and seat belts in the mid-sixties; and safer seats and numerous anti-pollution devices in the early seventies. All of these improvements are important. Entirely aside from what the advertising says, automobiles really do become safer and more reliable — not year by year, you may be sure, but decade by decade.

But not more comfortable, and certainly not better adapted to human needs. If you are over forty, think back to the first car you owned; and if you are under forty and somehow have access to an automobile made 20 or 25 years ago, get into it — and sit and reflect. No gymnastic ability whatever was required to enter the car or to leave it; and even arthritic passengers — and there are millions of them — could make it with comparatively little pain. You had the option of wearing a hat if you wished, and it didn't get squashed or knocked awry. You sat upright, and your feet were undisputably lower than your rump. The wall beside you did not close in at shoulder level; and in the back seat there was room for human feet, even large ones. You did not get a lap full of water when you opened the door on a rainy day. There was room enough, even in a conventional sedan, to carry some pretty bulky packages and even small items of furniture, and the trunk was almost cubical in interior shape, and designed like a real trunk — a space into which you could fit items of many different sizes and shapes. True, the rear door of a station wagon would swing open only one way, not two ways or six — but once it swung open you could get something big through it and into the cargo space: a mattress or box-spring, a dinette table, or perhaps even an armchair or a small sofa.

As we ponder that car of yesteryear we may well ask just who has benefited from the progressive squashing-down of the profile of our automobiles. Who is better off, now that we need the help of both hands and arms to enable us to enter or leave an automobile, and our legs must ride in a virtually horizontal position, and we sit so low that we can feel the chill of the pavement on a cold day, and we have to look upward to see over the wheel of a truck we may be passing on the highway? Who is better off, really, if the driver of a bus or truck doesn't even know we are there? Who is better off, now that we are so low that the air coming in for us to breathe is scooped up at a level just a few inches above the exhaust pipes of our neighbors?

And can we expect that designers in the future will

take into account any more than those of the past the human frame and the normal transportation needs of human beings? Of course not. No sane person would argue, on the basis of past performance, that cars will become more reasonable and more sensible in the years to come. Quite the contrary; unless the customers insist on something different, the designers and the manufacturers and the advertising fraternity will continue doing precisely what they have been doing in the past — promoting discontent with our present cars all the while that they are smothering us in sanctimonious explanations of just how they are serving us better by reducing the thickness of the metal they are using, by eliminating the spare tire, by scuttling the ventilator windows, by requiring us to buy headlight bulbs that cost over twice as much as the old ones, by eliminating instruments, and in ways too variegated to enumerate, by applying their ever-advancing engineering skills to the saving of a penny here and a penny there, and their market-research skills to the study of us the consumers, to see how much short-changing we will put up with.

And the technological improvements over the past 30 years, although real enough, have come along so slowly that no single improvement has rendered obsolete the car that doesn't have it, as the self-starter did, or the electric headlight. Only in the slow accumulation of improvements, over a period of 15 or 20 years, can new cars be said to be technologically superior to their predecessors. And in some respects, as for example sturdiness, reliability, and comfort, cars that are 10 or 12 or even 15 years old can look down their noses at the car that was brand new just last month.

These things will change only when we the consumers insist that they change. Consumers insist by buying or not buying. If we decline to buy the new model that cramps us physically more than the car we have now, or that has a gimmicky new kind of headlight or headlight eyelid, or that requires a water pump or fuel pump or carburetor or alternator that is merely different

from — not demonstrably superior to — the corresponding items on last-year's model, then these changes-for-
the-sake-of-change will gradually go out of favor with
the automobile companies — if there are enough of us.
If we insist, by buying or not buying, we will be able over
a lifetime, or perhaps only a decade, to persuade at least
one automobile manufacturer, domestic or foreign, to
deliver an automobile designed for the long term, not
merely the coming three or four years; and once one
manufacturer offers such an automobile and it is com-
mercially successful, all of the others will demonstrate
their leadership by doing the same thing.

All this is for the future. The present stretches out
ahead. There is no need to devote our lives and our
fortunes to the enlightening of tycoons in Detroit. We
have an automobile, thank you; you only offer us something less satisfactory. We can free our minds of all
thought of new cars, and think only of the small things
we must do to continue on and on with what we have.
By all means let us know when you have something
worth our while, Detroit.

We can wait.

5. WASTE ON A NATIONAL SCALE

Millions of worn-out automobiles go to the junk yard every year that in fact are not worn out at all. A few cars in any junk yard have been wrecked beyond reasonable repair, and a handful are there because they have become technologically obsolete; but rare indeed is the junked automobile that is worthless except as scrap metal. Most of the occupants of the junk yard were structurally sound when they were dragged through the gate. An inventory of serviceable components in that yard would be overwhelming: power trains, suspension systems, starting motors, alternators, brake systems, steering systems, ignition systems, instruments, lighting systems — the junk yard is a gold mine of sophisticated, ingenious mechanisms, each one awaiting the attention of the "compactor" that will convert it to a few cubic inches of densified waste that is suitable to feed to the steel furnaces.

If you were to stand at the junk yard gate and select the first car that came through that was not obviously smashed up, you would have an excellent chance of selecting an automobile that could be rendered serviceable and satisfactory with the expenditure of a few

hundred dollars. The one hulk you select may need an
engine overhaul and perhaps an additional major repair
job or two or even three; but to do all these things plus
the superficial things that would be required for comfort
and satisfaction would cost only hundreds of dollars —
not the thousands of dollars you take in stride when you
sign up for a new car.

The idea of snatching an automobile from the junk
yard gate is more likely to be fantasy than reality in the
lives of most readers of this book. Not so in the case of
the authors: there are two automobiles in our family
service right now that were in effect intercepted by us on
their way to the junk yard, and both are serving well.

The older and more spectacular and less defensible
of the two is a 1962 Cadillac that we bought in 1970 for
$350, knowing full well at first glance that if it offered
nothing else, it would at least put our ideas about rehabilitation to the test. We had Reliable Old Bert re-
habilitate it piecemeal, to the extent of $900 over a
period of several months, whereupon we made a
10,000-mile trip across the continent and back. (At the
farthest point away from home, in Seattle, we had $74
worth of generator trouble.) We don't know how far the
old car had traveled before we bought it, but from the
condition of the engine when we overhauled it 50,000
miles later, we concluded it had gone at least 217,000
miles by that time, and quite possibly 317,000. (The
odometer now reads 55,000 — so the total is now either
255,000 or 355,000 miles.) We have taken short trips
without number in this elderly automobile, and in addition to the 10,000-mile transcontinental trip, we made
another journey of 8,000 miles, and a third of 3,000
miles. We expect to make many another major trip in
the Cadillac over the coming five or even ten years.

The other car is a 1964 Ford Falcon that we bought
for $140 when it was ten years old. The engine emitted
a scream of protest when it ran, and the car shuddered
alarmingly as it got under way, either forward or in reverse. The owner, a pleasant woman, told us it needed a

new water pump and a new clutch. Indeed it did. Also, as R.O. Bert found, it needed new shock absorbers, upper ball joints, and a few new components of the steering gear. All this cost $535. The little Falcon now runs as smoothly as a sewing machine, and we would confidently set off on a transcontinental trip in it — but not enthusiastically, so jaded are our tastes after riding in Cadillac comfort these many years.

These two cars probably represent the extremes of cost of buying/rehabilitating/maintaining an automobile in indefinite service. We paid $675 for the Falcon and the immediate remedial work. (All money amounts here, as elsewhere in the book, are in terms of current dollars.) Repairs over the ensuing two years cost $21.56 per month, or $259 per year.

The Cadillac has cost much more, not only because it is a Cadillac, but also because it had traveled at least a hundred thousand miles more than the Falcon before it entered our lives. It cost the considerable total of $1,250 to buy and rehabilitate up to the time we left for Seattle. Repairs and further rehabilitation over the ensuing four-and-a-half years cost $58 per month, or $696 per year. Included among the repair bills have been a complete engine overhaul and major repairs to the differential, the steering gear, and the power unit in the braking system.

The newest car in our family — a 1966 Ford Galaxie, bought new — now registers 148,000 miles. It, too, has taken a trip around the United States: it was eight years old at the time, traveled 15,000 miles before it reached home again, and was driven the whole way by two young women, 20 years old. They, or we, would not hesitate to start out in it again tomorrow.

All these cars are serviceable, reliable, comfortable, and safe. Of all these qualities, safety is the most crucial and the most worrisome to people who have had no experience with older cars. And yet they have only to look around them: cars like our own cruise the highways all the time; we see them every time we go out — not

Classic Cars kept like gems, carefully polished and brought out only on special occasions for display, but old-shoe automobiles, in all stages of exterior preservation, traveling smoothly and carrying recent inspection stickers testifying to safe brakes and steering systems. And all around us are many thousands of service cars in daily use — taxicabs, police cars, delivery trucks, utility vans — that are driven several hundred thousand miles each, and no one thinks anything of it. And not even the automobile manufacturers, as eager as they are to persuade us to turn in our still-serviceable cars on new models, try to tell us that our older cars are not safe. Nowhere in any owner's manual or shop manual we have ever seen is there any intimation that it is risky to keep a car for a long time, so long as it is kept in good condition. During World War II the average age of cars that were scrapped was 18 years. The Motor Vehicle Manufacturers Association states in its official publication that American cars can last for 10 years or 100,000 miles without *any* kind of major overhaul, and that the factors that determine the age of cars on the road are the owners' attitudes, their ability to buy new cars, and the availability of new cars. Life expectancy is never mentioned as a factor.

And yet we toss automobiles on the junkheap by the millions every year that average only 12 years from the production line and are still good for many more years of service. It is an obscene act of irresponsibility and wastefulness.

It is worth considering what would happen if we stopped doing that, if gradually over a period of 10 or 15 years the American public developed sane attitudes and buying habits and above all more sensible maintenance practices with regard to their automobiles, and thereby increased the life-expectancy of American cars from 12 years to, say, 20.

An early casualty of such a development would be the Annual Model. If the American public in general

were ever to realize that change is not necessarily improvement, and in fact as often as not is retrogression,
automobile manufacturers would go along. They lead
the public where they think the public wants to go.

The passing of the Annual Model would bring other
benefits. Chief among these would be gradual liberation
from the tyranny of replacement parts that now costs the
public millions of dollars a year. In this area of replacement parts there is even more needless waste than in the
automobiles themselves.

The situation is this: thanks to changes in automobile design that manufacturers dictate every year,
almost every crucial part of each model of each automobile of each model-year is unique. Except for the
all-purpose nuts and bolts and most of the light bulbs,
the way to bet is that no part of your automobile is
interchangeable with the corresponding part in your
neighbor's car, unless the two cars are the same model
of the same year of the same make.

We are so accustomed to this insanity that most of
us are not even aware of it, and in fact we tend to think
of the automobile industry as the pioneer in developing
the concept of interchangeable parts. But if we compare
it with another important part of the economy, the electrical equipment industry, we see clearly what a
madhouse the replacement-parts business really is. By
1920, the manufacturers of electrical equipment had
standardized almost everything they produced: light
bulbs, plugs, switches, conduits, connection boxes,
fuses. In the ensuing decades, as new equipment was
developed, the manufacturers continued to standardize
each item. The result of all this is that when you need a
wall switch, you don't need to know who made your
equipment, or what year it was made, or by what catchy
name it is called; you simply go to the hardware store, or
a 5&10, or the housewares department of the supermarket, and buy a wall switch, knowing that it will fit
your system. Inventory and storage costs are kept at a
minimum. So are prices.

Not so with the fuel pump for your car. For 1966-model cars alone, for example, a popular mail-order catalog lists 11 different fuel pumps for General Motors cars, six for Ford cars, three for American Motors cars, and two for Chrysler cars — a total of 22 different pumps for the 1966 models of four companies.

It is not that these cars need different kinds of fuel pumps. A single design could cover the whole range of pumping demands, as witness the fact that the huge Lincoln engine and the smallest Ford Falcon require the same pump. In addition, all 22 pumps are operated by exactly the same kind of cam inside the engine, are bolted onto the engine in exactly the same way, and are hooked into the gasoline lines, both in and out, in precisely the same manner.

This insane — or deliberately contrived — situation means that suppliers of automobile parts must stock 22 different kinds of fuel pumps for one model year alone. For 10 model-years, which is the period that the manufacturers themselves make replacement parts available, a supplier must either keep on hand something in the neighborhood of 200 kinds of fuel pumps, or he must order them when they are needed, and the buyers must wait. A major mail-order supplier, whose list is by no means exhaustive, stocks 292 different fuel pumps.

Think of the cost of this crazy — or contrived? — situation to the car owner! The inventory and storage costs alone are enormous; and all down the line, from the designer, to the manufacturer, to the shipper, to the supplier, to the garage mechanic, profits are added to the price. And finally, we are the ones who pay for it all.

Are the automobile manufacturers making a deliberate effort to fleece the public as a matter of company policy? Not necessarily. The situation is more likely an unthinking but inevitable result of our national commitment to the Annual Model. A cosmetic or a gimmicky change made so that this year's model can be distinguished from last year's often makes it necessary to change other things to accommodate the gimmick.

Thus, if the stylists dictate that the windshield wiper blades must be recessed in the cowl, then the wiper/washer motor must be relocated and will probably have to be redesigned; and a change in the wiper/washer motor may make it necessary to re-orient or even redesign the power brake unit so it will fit into the new space. The stylists and the engineering designers and their bosses accept all this with equanimity. Since the new model is going to be manufactured in quantities of hundreds of thousands, the cost of redesigning a new fuel pump, or fan, or carburetor, or whatever, spread out over the whole huge production run, will come to only a few cents per unit, and sales emphasis can be put on the word *new*.

But the public suffers the consequences. First, each new design, each relocation, introduces the possibility of unforeseen hazards, difficulties, exasperations, and expense that will become known only later, after thousands of people have spent millions of dollars on these new cars. The gasoline line that connects the relocated fuel pump to the redesigned carburetor may have an unforeseen tendency to become detached and spray gasoline over the hot engine, thus developing notoriety as an incendiary missile. Or the accelerator-pedal pushrod to the relocated carburetor may turn out to be susceptible of jamming against a relocated hose, causing the car to forge ahead at full speed when the driver expects it to slow down. And then these cars must be recalled before they kill any more people, and the lucky ones who weren't killed can be grateful that all they have been called upon to suffer is anger and expense. (For more details about recent recalls, see page 49.)

But even if such major adversities are avoided, the cost to the public of the cosmetic and gimmicky changes is enormous. None of the redesigned components will fit previous models of the same car, so complete stocks of the new components must be built up in the thousands of warehouses and retail outlets throughout the country. In addition to the cost of this operation, there is another aspect: each new, non-interchangeable part that a parts

supplier adds to his stock creates additional pressure to
drop other parts for want of room and working capital.
Hence, replacement parts for earlier models become
more and more difficult to find.

With the arrival on the automobile scene of some
modicum of common sense, our society would be able
to decrease the number of new cars we manufacture
every year. Under the present circumstances, where 10
million new cars are made in a normal year and almost
as many are tossed on the junk heap, an increase of
eight years in the life of the average car would mean that
we would need only six million new cars a year. This
would save four million cars a year, which translates into
at least $18 billion, and immeasurable but colossal sav-
ings in natural resources and energy.

In the matter of energy alone, consider: to manufacture an automobile, iron ore and coal must be dug
out of the ground, using substantial amounts of energy
in the process. The raw materials must then be transported to a steel mill, behind a locomotive that burns up
more energy; they must be made into steel by a process
which uses enormous amounts of energy; this steel must
then be transported, behind another energy-consuming
engine, to fabricating plants, where it is made into parts
(using energy) that are then transported to assembly
plants (using additonal energy). Copper ore, likewise,
must be dug out of the ground (ditto); sand, too, dug up
and transported (ditto, ditto); petroleum or other chemical raw materials must be found and brought to the
surface (ditto, ditto) — all these for wire, insulation, upholstery, carpeting, paint, glass, light bulbs. After all
these things are assembled the finished product must
then be transported, a few at a time, on flat cars or
specially built trucks, to the dealers' showrooms — using
tremendous amounts of energy at each step of the way.

But the specific amounts of raw material and
energy we *use* to manufacture millions of automobiles annually, as enormous as they are, are not the

most significant facts about the automobile industry. The most important single aspect of it is that so much raw material and energy is *wasted*. There was a time when this seemed not to matter. We believed that our resources were limitless and that human progress could be measured in per-capita consumption of energy and raw materials: the more we used up, the better. And we were proud that we were the most ravenous consumers in the world. We now know that our resources are not limitless. Since panic swept across the globe when everyone first realized that oil is not forever, numerous plans and projects have been introduced to save us from disaster. Some of them may actually do so, eventually. In the meantime, and probably for the foreseeable future, one concept is paramount: conservation. We cannot begin to face the energy problems of the world and cope with them until we change by 180° our attitudes and practices. Instead of throwing things away, we must conserve them. And in this country, one of the first places to start is with the automobiles we already own.

Some argue, and the multitudes parrot the argument, that our society cannot afford to moderate its ravenous appetite for new cars because our entire economy depends upon the health of the automobile industry, and a healthy automobile industry means a healthy economy. In the United States, the motor vehicle industry provides almost 15 million jobs, these people point out, and a total payroll of the order of $120 billion a year. It consumes over 23 percent of all the steel consumed in the country, and almost 18 percent of the aluminum. Collectively, the companies and workers engaged in the manufacture and feeding and servicing of motor vehicles and the building and maintaining of roads pay over to the tax collector 25 percent of all Federal tax dollars and 16 percent of all state tax dollars; and the purchasers of automobiles do business with the consumer banking and credit industry to the extent of $89 billion every year. Conventional wisdom is that if the automobile industry were to stop growing, or even worse — horror of horrors! — grow smaller, our economy and everyone in it would be mortally stricken with economic stagnation. In this conventional view we could not as a nation afford to reduce our consumption of automobiles to a paltry six million a year.

This is yet another great American automobile myth. The economic consequence of prolonging automobile life expectancy from 12 years to 20 would be to expand the genuinely productive effort of the country by about $63 billion a year. If eight million new automobiles would serve our needs as satisfactorily as 12 million, then the difference of 4 million automobiles per year represents sheer waste. And this waste requires about $26 or even $28 billion every year in human effort to manufacture, distribute, and sell. The remainder of that $63 billion would be released by the consumer banking and credit industry: the pace of automobile selling and re-selling would be reduced in the same proportion that each owner's average period of ownership of each car increased. The present-day $89 billion per year of credit extended by the industry for the purchasing of automobiles would be reduced by about 40 percent, or about $36 billion. This colossal resource of credit would not be lost; like the $26 - $28 billion per year no longer wasted by the automobile producers/ distributors/sellers, it would be diverted to the production of things and services the people need more urgently than wasted automobiles.

This great American automobile myth, like the other myths we have lived by, gains credibility from what is not said. Most of the numbers the myth-makers provide are true. Huge numbers of people are indeed employed, and huge sums of tax money are indeed generated, and payrolls beyond the imagination of ordinary mortals are indeed maintained, by the automobile and all who serve it and use it. But the myth-makers give us only part of the story. If we wasted four million fewer automobiles per year than we do now, the country would still travel as many miles per year by automobile as it does now. The filling stations would still be just as busy. The highway lobby would still be just as active as it is now, and we would be building roads at just as high a rate. Repair shops and insurance offices would perform the same function they perform now, on about their present scale of operations; and we would all pay taxes on the gasoline we use and the licenses and permits we have to buy. Whether the steering wheel we sit behind is five years old or 25 would not affect these expenditures at all.

It is no more rational to manufacture automobiles we do not need than to manufacture anything else we do not need. If the myth-makers were urging us to support the manufacture of buggy-whips to the extent of $63 billion per year we would drown them in laughter. If they turned their attention to the economic benefits of employing a huge work force to dig holes in the ground, and a second work force to follow them and fill up the holes again, we would see the lunacy of it — however vocal the support of the shovel-manufacturers' and the work-glove-producers' associations.

No responsible member of our society would urge the immediate curtailment of any segment of the economy to the extent of $63 billion per year. The dislocations and repercussions would cause terrible human suffering and economic upheaval, and it would be many years before stability could be restored. But immediate curtailment of the production of automobiles is not a likely catastrophe. A truly massive business recession can cause some cut-back in automobile buying, as indeed it did in 1975; but sales bounced back again the next year. Any permanent change in the buying habits of automobile owners will come slowly, over a long period. Someday, perhaps, we will all own our cars twice as long as we are in the habit of owning them now; this is an idea that may ultimately prevail. But it is an idea that will start small, with a handful of people who are fed up, and it will spread only gradually, as is the wont of good ideas. There is always plenty of time for the economy to adjust to the invasion of common sense.

The buggy-whip analogy is jocular, as it has been for generations, but it was no joke to the people who were in the buggy-whip business 75 years ago. And there are other analogies. In 1920, the U.S. rail industry employed a work force of 2 million people; today it is 500,000, a reduction of 75%. (In 1978, the motor vehicle and equipment manufacturers employed only 977,100 people.) What happened to all those railroad workers? What happened to all those thousands of people who manned and womanned those trans-Atlantic and trans-Pacific ocean liners as recently as 15 years ago? Whatever happened to all of those skilled stone-masons — the young ones — of the thirties?

These are not difficult questions. Everybody knows the answer. Attrition is the primary factor that reduces a potential nightmare to a normal evolutionary phenomenon. The elderly buggy-whip worker saw it happening, and his sons migrated to Detroit. These same sons will watch the automobile industry for the benefit of their own sons and — nowadays — daughters.

Entirely new industries will appear, as they always have. It is conceivable — it is inevitable — that thousands of young people who might grow up to work on automobile production lines will do something better with their lives than producing automobiles the world doesn't really need, and that it would be very much better off without.

6. BUT REPAIRS ARE SUCH A HASSLE!

When you start up in the morning, the engine takes forever to catch. The filling station boss says you need a tune-up. O.K., tune 'er up: $70, give or take a few. A week later, the car jiggles in a suspicious way every time you back out of the driveway. You call Reliable Old Bert; he says bring 'er in for transmission adjustments and new transmission fluid and filter. So you do, and it costs $40. Six weeks go by, and suddenly at a traffic light the whole front of the car is enveloped in a cloud of steam. The radiator hose has failed. Into the nearest service station for a new hose and a gallon of antifreeze to replace what spewed out: $20. Then, the very next day, the starter gives you heart failure: it goes "click" when you turn the key. On the third try the starter works, but you know you're in trouble, so back to Reliable Old Bert. New starter solenoid: about $40. That's life, you tell yourself through your teeth. Except three days later it does it again. Back to Bert, and this time he replaces the whole starter, and the cost of the job is now up to $110 to say nothing of some weakening of your faith in R.O. Bert.

But at least your troubles are behind you, until the

muffler goes, a month or two later, or the exhaust pipe, or the resonator, or the tail pipe . . .

How much of this tyranny can you put up with? Who's in charge here, anyway? You? or the bucketabolts? You know it's economical, sensible, and all that, to make do with the old car rather than buy a new one, but how about the worry, the uncertainty, the time, the inconvenience, and above all, the *exasperation* of Fighting the Good Fight? Besides, it isn't cheap to maintain this struggle. Those repairs add up. And anyway, one of the reasons you earn money is to make life easier and more pleasant, so if you have money for a new car why not buy one and get away from all these problems?

Once you get into this state of mind, it is safe to bet that you will soon be touring your local Automobile Row, looking at stickers and kicking tires and absorbing as best you can the pitches of the salesmen. And you will be embarked on a series of different Good Fights.

First comes The Choosing: which car do you want? Before you can make up your mind on this question, you have a lot of shopping to do, and a great many decisions to make. How powerful? (How much power do you need for your kind of driving? How much do you want? How much can you afford?) How big? (For the daily run to work? For the vacations with the whole family? Both?) Does color matter? Manual or automatic transmission? What kind of suspension? Radial tires? The brakes — disc or drum? Power brakes? Power steering and windows? Air conditioning? Automatic speed control? Automatic headlight dimmers? Some of these items are optional on some cars and not on others. If they are optional, how much do they add to the cost? Are they worth it? Or not?

At the same time, you need to be thinking about The Financing, unless you have a bunch of money squirreled away. And not only thinking — shopping around, and figuring, and considering interest rates, and different contracts — the terms of the financing, the length of the contract. You'll need to talk to the dealer, whose contract may turn out to be the most expensive, to your bank and other banks about personal loans on your savings or your life insurance, to your union, your fraternal lodge, the AAA, your credit union.

Also, after you make up your mind on some of the basic items but before you sign a contract, you should get the best possible bargain from the dealer you will probably be buying from. This will involve some specialized shopping around, and it may demand a demonstration of a toughness that may not come easy.

Some of this elaborate ritual is enjoyable to some people, but it takes a lot of time at best, and you cannot honestly consider that you're leaving problems behind you when you abandon your present car for a new one. You're simply exchanging your present set of problems for a new set.

And you're not finished with the problems when you sign the contract and drive away from the show-room. If you are sensible, you will take the new car to your mechanic immediately and have him go over it carefully, and then take the car back to the dealer with a list of what's wrong with it. It's almost certain to have some new-car defects. In the April, 1976, issue of Consumer Reports, the editors reviewed a study of 36 new cars tested by Consumers Union engineers over the preceding year: they reported a total of 826 defects, an average of 23 per car. These were not design defects which would be the same with every car of the same make and model, but deficiencies caused by lapses on the assembly line or in dealer preparation of those specific cars. Not all the flaws were dangerous, but there were an average of five per car that were called "serious" by the engineers. In addition, the investigators found 692 cosmetic flaws not included in the list of defects — paint bubbles, misfit trim, dribbling adhesive, and so on — which came to an average of 19 per car.

At this stage you embark on the Warranty Fight. Your experience may be a relatively pleasant one, if you're lucky in the particular new car you have bought, and the particular dealer you bought it from. On the other hand, your experience may be disagreeable in the extreme. Although some dealers are willing to make good on flaws in the cars they sell and do so promptly, by and large, warranty work is not profitable to dealers, and they have minimal desire to lavish costly shop time on cars they have already sold. The dealer's interest is best served not by repairing your car, but by talking you out of believing that he has any obligation to repair it. After you decide that you're not going to get satisfaction, you will then embark upon more heroic courses of action: call or write the factory zone manager, if he is listed in your owner's manual, and try to enlist his aid; write the factory, giving all the pertinent information and sending copies of all the relevant papers; send copies of all this to the attorney general of your state, your local department of consumer affairs, the Consumer Federation, the Consumers Union, and the Center for Auto Safety in Washington, D.C.; and perhaps take the whole matter to a small claims court.

Or more probably you will give up somewhere in the middle of this hassle and pay the bills yourself.

Help on the Hot Line (800) 424-9393

The National Highway Traffic Safety Administration has established a toll-free hot line to answer questions from consumers about their car problems. If the problem is with the manufacturer, a solution can be reached about half the time, according to an official of the agency. The office maintains a computerized file of information about specific makes and models of cars, and although they will not make judgments on the best kinds of cars to buy, they will answer specific questions, and will identify the 15 million or so cars on the road that have been the subject of manufacturer's recall and never had the safety defect corrected.

As uncomfortable and as time-consuming as all this would be, you could be unluckier still, if you choose a car that contains a basic design defect of such magnitude that all cars of that make and model are later recalled. These have come to be known as Detroit's Big Blunders. There was the Chevrolet with the broken engine mount that allowed the engine to lift out of position and jam the throttle or the brake; this car figured in a case against General Motors in which it was claimed that the car went out of control as a result of the defective engine mount and killed four people. The judgment against G.M. was for $600,372, and nearly 7 million Chevrolet V-8 cars and light trucks of the model years 1965 through 1969 were recalled. Nearly 150,000 Plymouths and Dodges were recalled in 1972 because of metal fatigue that could cause gasoline leaks at the fuel filter—a clear fire hazard. More than three and a half million Chevrolets, Pontiacs, Oldsmobiles, and Buicks were ordered recalled in 1973 because of a design defect that made it possible for gravel to lodge in the steering system and render it impossible to turn the wheel to the left. A pin was just possibly missing in the steering systems of 58,000 '73 Torinos. A misalignment in the throttle of '73 and '74 Torinos, Mavericks, Montegos, Comets, and Cougars could cause the throttle to stick in the open position. The 1973 Pontiacs were subject to a fuel disorder which could allow fuel to flow out on the ground—another fire hazard. And some of the '73 Ford Torino Rancheros with power steering were liable to loss of control in the steering.

There is another category of new-car hassle: this is the Detroit Blunder that does not have to be recalled because its deficiencies are not murderous, but only maddening and expensive. There is the car so designed that it will cost you $150 instead of the usual $50 to replace the front shock absorbers; another with an aluminum engine that has a tendency to overheat and destroy itself, with replacement costing between $600 and $700 and maybe the manufacturer will replace it and maybe he won't; still another in which some of the nuts that maintain the wheel alignment keep coming loose, a problem that Consumer Reports called "a nasty front-suspension defect;" and yet one more with a paint job so inadequate that the car will long be remembered for the spectacularly high rate at which its body disintegrated from rust.

Meanwhile, the car you turned in on a new one (in order to avoid the hassle of repairs, you remember) will perhaps have been bought by someone else at a ridiculously low price. If that buyer has the good sense to get off to a good start, the chances are that he or she will conclude eventually that it was a smart and lucky buy. A good start involves having the car checked over from front bumper to rear, replacing parts that need replacing, adjusting components that need adjusting, and enlisting the mechanic's help in deciding what repairs and replacements will have to be made when.

If you want to, you can do the same thing with that car. At your point of desperation, when you decided to get rid of it because repairs were such a hassle, a good mechanic could have foreseen almost all the problems that were in store for you during the coming months, and forestalled them. You would only have had to ask him to make a thorough examination and authorize him to adjust, repair, or replace not only the components that needed attention, but also everything that was likely to fail within the next few months.

Forestall *all* the problems? No. In the first place, if you have lived with automobiles long enough to have a healthy superstition about them, you know that a sinister force enters your life the minute you spend any sizable sum on auto repairs. This sinister force sees to it that several other things go wrong, one after the other, presumably to test your character on some higher occult level. And aside from adversity of this irrational kind, other things will go wrong that you or your mechanic should have foreseen but didn't.

But forestall *most* of the problems? Yes. You will

have to make up your mind first of all to do a thorough job of it, either from the beginning with a new car, or from this point on with an older car—which is just as feasible, and cheaper. You will have to find a mechanic you are comfortable with, taking into account not only his competence but also his availability and his judgment and his personality. And regardless of the age of the car you will also have to accept the inconvenience of scheduled maintenance work, and of being deprived of the car on those days—keeping firmly in mind during those periods that having anything done to your car is more trouble than not have anything done to it; but also that having work done at your convenience is better than having it done at your inconvenience.

Of all these requirements, the most difficult is making up your mind to do a thorough job of it. It isn't easy to ask a mechanic to replace a fuel pump at 75,000 miles when it is working perfectly well, especially when the mechanic tells you he has known lots of fuel pumps that lasted a lot longer than 75,000 miles; and it is even less easy to spend $500 or $600 on an engine overhaul, or $400 on body work, or $100 on seat covers and carpeting, for a car that you couldn't sell for more than $300 in the insane automobile market. But if you make up your mind to do a thorough job, you will find yourself with a satisfactory, operating automobile.

Repairs are indeed a nuisance. Nothing that anyone can say or do will change that basic fact. But buying a new car is time-consuming, hard work, and expensive, with no guarantee whatever that after you have spent all that time, energy, and money, you will be free of hassle.

You have a choice, it appears: on the one hand, the frying pan; on the other hand, the fire. The real problem, which comes after the choice is made, is to arrange life so that the heat is bearable.

If you should choose to keep your present car and forgo the dubious pleasures of buying a new car, you will find in the rest of this book some help in doing that with as little disruption and exasperation as possible.

7. THE CASE FOR KEEPING A NOTEBOOK

It is a good idea to keep a notebook, and at least one pencil that works, in the glove compartment of your car, and to enter into that notebook everything you put into or onto the car and everything you have done to it. After you try it for a while you may give it up — but try it. If you can stick with it, you will be glad you did.

Your primary guide to preventive maintenance is the Maintenance Schedule beginning on page 71. This schedule tells you what to do, and when. In theory, it should be a simple matter to follow the schedule. In practice, you will probably wonder, often, whether you actually did something the schedule calls for. Did you, for some reason, put off the scheduled wheel-alignment check six months ago? You may want to know how many miles' service your Brand Y tires on the front have given, and whether they lasted longer than the Brand X that preceded them. Your mechanic may want to know how often you have had to add water to the battery, so he can decide whether the voltage regulator needs adjusting. When did you last have the oil filter changed? Does the sticker on the door-jamb record the most recent oil change, or the one before that — or the one before that? Do radial tires actually yield better gasoline mileage in your car, or do they work wonders only in advertising copy? And is your gasoline mileage up where it used to be, or has it declined, thus suggesting the need of carburetor or distributor adjustments? Did you replace the antifreeze last fall or the fall before?

You may believe your shop receipts provide an adequate record, and sometimes they do, but more often the handwriting is illegible and the nomenclature incomprehensible. It is better to rely on your own notebook record than on something like "R & B (or is it R & R?) Ullmmo alejuin mtj, labor $15.00", and under "Parts and Supplies," "1 X57332B, 1 set 61942B2, 2 clamps." Do file your shop receipts, please, but don't count on them for anything more specific than the date the car was in the shop (if they remembered to record it) and the cost (which they did record).

The reasons for not keeping a notebook are also persuasive. It's more trouble to keep one than not — and who needs more trouble? Perhaps worse, a notebook is a myth-killer. Never again will you be able to believe that your car delivers 16 miles per gallon, based on your careful measurements on the fishing trip last year. Your notebook is all too likely to tell you that your gasoline mileage through the four seasons of the year averages out to 12.2 rather than 16; so you will have to remain silent when others start telling themselves and each other about their whopping gasoline mileages. If you are a notebook-keeper, you may check your odometer from time to time against highway mileposts — and thus record in the book that your odometer lies on the high side, and that your gasoline mileage is even worse than you thought. Another myth the notebook may dispel is the myth that repairs are eating you up, and so perhaps you should get a new car. The notebook may show that you have actually spent only $200 over the past year for repairs, and that the remainder of the $500 in garage bills actually went for tires, tune-ups, oil changes, and other things that a newer car would require just as frequently.

The notebook question is of course a question of being interested enough to take the trouble. We started keeping notebooks in 1942, and still keep them. We find the trouble of it to be negligible, and the information it supplies to be indispensable to our comfort about the automobile. We hope you will give it a try.

8. YOUR MECHANIC AND YOU

Behind every automobile that runs indefinitely is a working relationship between the owner and a competent, conscientious mechanic. It is important that you find such a mechanic. You may be lucky enough to know one already, but if not, you must inquire and shop around until you find one. They do exist, in greater numbers than you may believe.

The mechanic you need is old enough to have acquired wide experience, so it is not unreasonable to think of 35 as a minimum age. He — or perhaps she, 15 or 20 years from now — does not hand down diagnoses instantly, because he distrusts all instant diagnoses, including his own. He is conscientious about scheduling jobs, and only rarely fails to finish a job on time, and then because it, or one that had been scheduled earlier, turned out to be particularly difficult. His record in diagnosis and cure is certainly not perfect but it is good by the standards of the trade; and if you have to bring your car back for another try, he is neither indifferent to the earlier failure nor irritated at you for causing him further trouble. He strikes you as honest, by whatever standards you judge honesty. He understands your automobile priorities, and shares your views either completely or sufficiently so that you can work together. All in all, the mechanic you need is a mechanic you have confidence in and feel comfortable with.

If you are female, you may have the special problems of a female in a world that is considered by many of its inhabitants to be exclusively male. Some mechanics treat women customers either as hopeless idiots or as scatterbrains — cute but dumb. Some of this treatment, sad to say, is brought on by women themselves, who rarely take themselves seriously as owners and maintainers of their automobiles. "I don't really know anything about cars," they say apologetically. Or they even say, "My husband says it needs. . . ." Part of this posture comes from the ages-old way women have had, and some still have, of pretending weakness in order to elicit male strength and help. But much of it comes quite honestly from the fact that few women know much about cars and this fact diminishes their self-confidence when they talk to mechanics. What these women do not know is that few men know much about cars either, and that everybody, female or male, is capable of learning enough to talk sensibly to a mechanic.

There is no need for a woman to put up with being put down, and for a woman a sexist mechanic is impossible to deal with over an extended period in a satisfactory way. For that reason, a woman may have to hunt longer and harder for a mechanic than a man would have to do.

The service station you favor may be able to handle most minor maintenance jobs as competently as a full-service garage, and more conveniently for you. Beware, though, of the service station where the owner or manager "doesn't get involved with much repair work," but has "a good mechanic who really knows his stuff." At the filling-station level, don't count on anybody on the premises to be a better mechanic than the boss man.

If you must seek out a more satisfactory mechanic than any you know, you will probably go about it pretty much as you search for a doctor. You will ask around. Your service station manager can recommend garages to do jobs that are beyond his own capabilities, and your friends and acquaintances will usually be only too happy to tell you who they go to. The yellow pages of the telephone directory may be of some help; and there may be a dealer in your brand of automobile within feasible geographical range. Beyond these obvious suggestions, you will proceed pretty much on your own.

You may encounter some surprises. For example, one could reasonably expect the service department of a franchised dealer to be the most competent garage in town for maintaining the make of car the dealer handles. Thus, the mechanics in the service department of a Ford agency do concentrate on Fords, and they are likely to have any specialized tool that facilitates work on this component or that. The Ford dealer has every incentive to serve you well and at reasonable prices, so that he will have the inside track when you next shop for a new car. Often all of these expectations are borne out, and it is never unreasonable to sample the service department of a new-car dealer if you have no cogent reason for avoiding it.

Be as prepared for disappointment there as at any other garage, however, because other factors work against the dealer's garage. The owner of the establishment is primarily in the business of selling new cars. He may "know very little about mechanical work," and thus may govern the management of the service department entirely according to the service manager, the account books, and the complaint record. The department may be prosperous even though it is mediocre, thanks to the large number of owners who assume that it is the proper home for maintenance work, and think no more about it. And finally, the service department may charge substantially higher prices than other first-class garages because it must carry its share of the expenses of a large establishment at an expensive location.

Any mechanic you try on for size will necessarily be on trial for a while; and in all fairness, remember that you will be on trial too. You are looking for competence, good judgment, availability, and honesty; in his customers the mechanic is looking for reasonableness both in demands and in judgment of his work, and some degree of competence in describing symptoms. And both of you are looking for a person you can work with and trust over a period of years. This means that the mechanic will sometimes recommend the less expensive course of action if he believes it to be the proper one; and it means that you will have him do most of your work and you will buy most of your tires and batteries from him, even though now and then you can get better prices somewhere else.

In recent years vast amounts of poison have been pumped into the relationship between automobile mechanics and their customers. "Garages are robbing you blind" is the gleeful message of any number of books and polls and surveys. There are robbers abroad in the land, no doubt of that, in automobile repair shops as well as shops of all other kinds — including shops that publish books about robbers or about automobile maintenance. But you will be the loser if you let blind suspiciousness dominate your relationship with a self-respecting, competent garage. It can get along perfectly well without such customers.

Many competent mechanics simply do not subscribe to the concept of keeping a car running indefinitely. One of the best mechanics we have ever known steadfastly urged us not to "try to make a new one out of it." At the other extreme are mechanics, just as competent, who believe as firmly as we that new automobiles are primarily for playboys and suckers. The majority of mechanics are somewhere in between, each with his own views. The mechanic you work with may not fully agree with your intention to keep the car indefinitely — perhaps as long as another 15 or even 20 years; but he is not likely to question whether any specific routine repair is worth making, even though the car may by now be fairly elderly. This amount of agreement is all you need in normal circumstances. However, when the time comes to make a major repair — to do an engine overhaul, for example — on an elderly car, it may be necessary for you and your mechanic to have a heart-to-heart talk about the economics and the philosophy of the matter. If you have chosen your mechanic well, and have worked harmoniously with him over a reasonable period of time, he will not only be sympathetic, but will also be helpful.

Philosophical exchanges may also be needed in connection with some aspects of preventive maintenance. Mechanics tend to be more interested in repairing than in anticipating trouble. This preference doesn't extend to everything; it is conventional to inspect brake systems periodically and replace brake parts before they are worn out, and to replace ignition parts, and various belts and hoses, to forestall failure. But in connection with other components you may have to lead your mechanic through new territory if you follow the teachings of this book. It is not conventional to replace a fuel pump or a water pump or an alternator that is still working well, however long it has served and whatever your ideas about life-expectancy. Here again, if you have chosen your mechanic wisely, he will agree with you in substance, if perhaps not in degree; but you may have to explain to him several times, under several different circumstances, that it is worth the extra cost to you to replace components before they fail, to avoid a shutdown when they fail.

An important thing to recognize in your discussions with any mechanic is that although he may understand better than you the inner workings of your automobile, he is not for that reason alone a better judge of how long you should keep your car running, and whether or not it's worth doing. He has been subjected to the same barrage of sales pitches over the years as has the rest of

the public, and it may never have occurred to him until
you came along that it is possible to act counter to those
pitches. He is a mechanic, not an economist, nor a social
thinker, nor a reformer. "But I'm no economist, either,"
you may say, "nor a social thinker, nor a reformer."
Perhaps not; but you are a better judge — in fact, you
are the only competent judge — of your actions in connection with your automobile. So long as what you want
to do is mechanically possible — and your mechanic is
the man to tell you that — the decision about whether or
not to do it is yours, not his. If he is opposed to what you
want to do, then you need to find a mechanic who will
go along with you. Your major goal here is not to win an
argument with a mechanic, but to keep your car in satisfactory service.

   When you take your car in to your mechanic with a
mysterious symptom, you may be confronting him with
a difficult professional decision. Diagnosis of automobile
ailments is often uncertain, and even a superior
mechanic may not be sure of the cause of a problem.
Should he, then, replace all the components that might
be causing the trouble and thereby charge you for some
unnecessary work? Or should he begin with the most
likely possibility, replace that single component, and
thereby risk missing the trouble and causing you to
come back, perhaps several times? An important factor
here is that a substantial portion of the mechanic's profit
comes from replacement parts, which he buys at
wholesale and sells to you at retail; he therefore has a
strong incentive to replace components on mere suspicion. This incentive is reinforced when he has a customer to whom it is more important to cure the ailment
quickly than to save a little money. On the other hand,
no mechanic would want to lose you as a customer
because you think he is extravagant.
   You can help your mechanic in this dilemma by
conveying to him as clearly as possible your own general
preference regarding repair cost versus repair certainty.

You may not be able to do this all at once, but over a period of several visits the two of you can come to some understanding of the way you prefer to do business. You probably won't want to encourage him to spend your money with abandon, but if in general you like the more comprehensive and expensive treatment in the interests of convenience, you should let him know that. If, on the other hand, you are interested most of all in saving money and don't mind spending some time and convenience in exchange, let him know that.

You can help your mechanic make up his mind on this matter, too, by being as specific as possible in describing symptoms. You don't tell him much when you say, "It clunks," or "It feels as if the wheels are about to come off." It's better to say something like, "The engine jerks when I accelerate," or "Something in the back whines when I turn a corner to the left," or "Something up front goes clack-clack when I go over a rough spot." These are more specific; they attempt to define the problem in terms of its location, the time of its appearance, and its specific quality.

You can help your relationship with your mechanic in another way: by not blaming him personally for the outrageous increases in the prices of replacement parts. When you discover that a power-steering belt, for example, now costs eight dollars, it does no good whatever to bellow that the man's robbing you. Chances are he's charging you the normal price for it — that is, the cost to him from his supplier plus a conventional mark-up. He may even agree with you that the price is outrageous. But there's not much he can do about it, and if you turn the air blue with your comments, he may respond by being too busy to take care of you next time you come in.

The only reasonable treatment for a sudden attack of indignation about the rising costs of replacement parts is to take a brief tour of the nearest new-car lot; this may cause you to reflect that although eight dollars for a belt is indeed a huge increase over last time, $7,300 for a car that not long ago sold for $6,750 is not only an enormous increase, it's a lot more dollars.

There are two varieties of disappointment that seem to be especially connected with mechanics. The first is the mechanic who performs fairly well for several visits, thus getting your hopes up that perhaps you have found someone you can stick with, and then turns out not to be satisfactory at all.

The second kind of disappointment hurts more: this comes about if Reliable Old Bert prospers as he should in a just world. Customers beat a path to the door of a superior mechanic, and he must be strong-minded and wise indeed not to expand his operation beyond what he can handle. The time may come when Bert has two or three mechanics to help him, and Bert is no longer a mechanic but the manager of a business; and even though he is a first-class mechanic, he may turn out to be a third-class business manager. In any case, Bert no longer works on your car — one of the boys does that. And indeed, Bert may be so busy dealing with customers in person and on the phone that he cannot even participate in the diagnosis of your car's ailments or the decision of what should be done. A situation like this usually develops slowly, and it may take you some time to recognize it after it has developed; but when you do you will have to start searching again for a satisfactory mechanic — more in sorrow than in anger — and keeping firmly in mind that there really are good mechanics available in the land, and that you will find one.

9. THINGS YOU DON'T HAVE TO DO BUT WILL BE GLAD YOU DID IF YOU DO

One of the most expensive ideas you can have about an automobile is this: "The old heap has just about had it." The minute you begin thinking this way, you are well on the way to the purchase of a new car at a cost of four or five — or seven? — thousand dollars. Any amount of money it takes to prevent such a state of mind will be money well spent, since whatever you spend on your present car will be less than you would have to spend on a new car.

This book is intended chiefly to convey the idea that it is much cheaper and more sensible and less wasteful to keep your present car running superbly than it is to buy a new car. But running superbly may not be enough for you. You may also want a car that looks and feels comfortable and respectable. There is no need to put up with a car that has rust holes in the body, or a smashed trunk, or a door that sticks, or a window that whistles in the wind. There is no more reason to be indifferent to a shabby-looking car than a shabby-looking house. And it is no more difficult to keep your car's appearance to a high standard than it is to keep its running gear in superb condition.

The first requirement is a good hospital. Once you decide to wage war against shabbiness, you will need a body shop that is capable of providing a long-term, satisfying relationship. You go about finding one in the same way you search out a satisfactory mechanic: by asking your service-station man, your mechanic, and your accident-prone friends, and then getting acquainted with several body-shop proprietors or managers who appear to be worth the trouble. Beyond that, you will have to choose on the basis of how each one acts and sounds. And as in the case of choosing a mechanic, it is sensible to have the jobs done one at a time, at first, so that you can see how a shop performs on Job A before contracting for Job B and Job C. You may be able to save some money by having everything done at once, but until you can be confident that the work will be satisfactory, it is better to risk little than all.

Body shops pose a problem that is not shared by mechanics in general. Collision work provides most of their income, and most collision work is paid for by insurance companies rather than by individuals. Body-shop owners complain that insurance companies hammer them down unconscionably in price, but to the ordinary customer, some body shops seem to charge high prices and get away with it. It's sensible to shop around for price levels as well as for competence. If you find a body shop owner or manager who looks with sympathy on your plan to keep your car in good shape for a long time, chances are you've found a man who will be reasonable about prices.

Such a man is easier to find now than he was some years ago, and he may be easier to find in the future than he is now. As more and more people keep their cars longer and longer, the repair trade will doubtless respond with greater interest in non-insurance work. This trend may already have started, so don't judge body shops in general, or one shop in particular, on the basis of an experience you had 15 years ago.

Dents, Crumples and Bashes. Folk wisdom dictates that if an automobile has been in a serious accident, you shouldn't fool with it at all. This is nonsense, but it serves the insurance companies very well. The automobile "blue book" provides the insurance companies with a handy device: they manage to limit their liability for a car that has been in an accident by declaring it "totaled", and then paying the owner the wholesale price quoted in the current edition of the Blue Book. This is always a low price. The owner is not required to accept that settlement, but he or she is much less likely to fight it if "everybody knows" that a severly damaged automobile can never be made right again.

It is another American automobile myth. The fact is that repair shops cope all the time with bent frames, smashed doors, buckled hoods, crumpled radiators or air-conditioning cooling coils — whatever the horror, any self-respecting body shop, supplemented by a good mechanic, can put it right again.

If you have to have major work done on an elderly car, you may encounter in the body shop the same mentality that produces the Blue Book, and that you may already have found in your garage: "Well, all right, I'll do it, if you want to put all that money into a car that's only worth about $400." Over the years to come, body shops will probably begin to realize that your car is worth what it would cost you to replace it with something equally satisfactory. If it would cost $2700 to get another car as good as your present one, $550 for major rehabilitation is not exorbitant.

Dinging and Bumping are two operations commonly carried out on sheet metal. Dinging is the tap-tap-tapping of a light hammer on a mis-shapen area of sheet metal to encourage it to return to its original shape. Bumping is a somewhat more vigorous assault on a more seriously mis-shapen area, to bring it into the range of the more delicate dinging operation. Both are highly skilled jobs.

It is sometimes easier and therefore cheaper to replace a battered section of sheet metal on the body of your car than it is to repair it. Often a body shop will cut out a mangled or corroded section of fender or door and weld a new section of sheet metal into place. In many cases a whole panel such as the outer skin of a door can be purchased. Such replacement panels must ordinarily be ordered, and this takes time, but if you can wait for the part to arrive, this may be the best course to follow.

Body Solder (pronounced "sodder") is often used when it is not feasible to smooth out a crumpled surface by dinging; the repairman covers the area with solder and then shapes the layer of solder to the proper smoothness by filing and sanding.

There are two kinds of solder — genuine and plastic. Genuine solder is a mixture primarily of lead and tin; plastic solder is a mixture of lead powder and plastic putty. When it is skillfully applied, genuine solder will adhere indefinitely to even large areas of steel. The plastic substitute is all right for repairing small holes or for smoothing out small depressions, but over an area larger than a dime, its life-expectancy is comparatively short. Genuine solder is more expensive but it is well worth its additional cost. You should let your repairman know that you want a permanent repair, not one to merely last until you trade in the car.

Rust — Early and Late. *Early rust* is that first brown stain that you will probably try to ignore, but shouldn't. If you will have someone go over it right away, you will head off the trouble before it amounts to anything. The basic problem is almost always the primer coat. Modern lacquers and enamels for metal are superb; but if the primer coat is inadequate, then the superb finish coat is no more protective than whitewash would be. Whenever a brown spot appears, it tells you that the primer coat has not adhered to the steel at that spot. Water has penetrated both the surface coat and the primer and attacked the steel, and rust has soaked back through the moisture in the coatings. It is important to act promptly on brown-spot warnings if you want to prevent the next step, late rust.

Late rust is what follows when you ignore early rust, and although it is more challenging, it is no cause for despair. And it is certainly no cause for spending thousands of dollars for a new car. Even very large holes in fenders, doors, and other sheet-metal parts can be repaired; body shops do it all the time.

The Rusty Bumper poses a singular problem because chromium plating cannot be applied by spraying or brushing, and you can't just side-step the problem by painting the bumper because paint won't stick to chromium plating. Bumpers can be re-plated at moderate cost; if new bumpers are still available for your car, it may be less expensive to replace than to re-plate.

Exterior Trim. You will almost certainly suffer mishap to a chrome strip or two or three, over the years. Generally speaking, precise replacements are available for the first 10 years; after that, replacement is more difficult, but not impossible. The precise item for your car may not be available, but any competent body shop can provide acceptable alternatives. If worse comes to worst, the shop can remove all signs of the original trim strips and the fixtures they were fastened to, fill up the holes, and provide a smooth shiny surface with no memory of trim at all. This is often an improvement.

A Complete Paint Job can work wonders in the appearance of an automobile and the spirits of its owner. This should not be surprising, since we paint houses and boats and furniture in the expectation that the paint job will improve things. But we seem to put cars in a different category; somehow we expect a re-painted car to look sleazy. It doesn't have to. A good paint job will do as much as anything to make your car look loved and cared-for, and make you feel pleased and proud.

You can paint it the same color it was when it was

new if that interests you. The paint formula is identified on an information tag on your car, and paint of that same formula will be available at any serious supplier of automobile parts.

If you want a different color, select one from the range offered by an automobile company; don't buy it from a general paint store. Automobile manufacturers publish their paint formulas and matching paint can be supplied by auto-parts shops at any time in the reasonable future. The same cannot be said of paints supplied by a general paint store or hardware store. **Be sure to record** the number of the formula where you will be able to find it in the future. One of the best reasons for repainting with the original paint formula is that you will always know where to find the paint record.

Interior Lights — instrument lights, dome lights, trunk lights, map lights, under-hood lights — are replaceable at modest cost. When they go out, as they eventually will, replace them promptly. They are a convenience and it's foolish to do without them when you can have them so readily.

Windows and Doors. The windshield may leak around the edges; the door may drag on something when you open it; the window may rattle when it is half-way down; you may have to slam the door harder than you used to; the wind may whistle through the weatherstripping.

All of these can be repaired easily and at moderate cost. Glass replacement is routine, window and windshield gaskets are replaceable, the window mechanism ditto, and ditto the felt channel the window rides in. Power windows almost never balk, but if they do all parts can be replaced with advance warning to the body shop to give them time to order. Door clearance and drag are adjustable; no need even to install new parts. Minor repairs usually restore to good health hinges and the swing-check devices that hold doors open, but even if total replacement is needed, they don't cost much.

Upholstery and Carpeting. Automobile slip covers range from sleazy to superb, with sidelines into garish and gaudy. But the important point is that without risking bankruptcy you can buy seat covers that will last from two to six times as long as the original upholstery. Carpeting, too, is available, and even the interior ceiling (it's called the "headliner") and the upholstery on the insides of the doors ("interior door panels") can be replaced at moderate cost.

Interior Moving Parts. The primary enemy of heater blowers, air-conditioner units, adjustable seats, radios, ashtrays, cigar lighters, glove compartment doors, and knobs of all kinds is the tendency of owners to be philosophical about their misbehavior or disappearance. By all means be stoic if it pleases you; but you don't have to put up with any of these adversities if they irritate you. The heater blower probably has a worn-out switch or a blown fuse. The air conditioner may need a charge of refrigerant or perhaps a new expansion-valve diaphragm. The driver's seat may become difficult to move forward and backward as the car gets on in years, but your service-station people can clean the tracks and squirt lubricant into the works and put it all back in smooth service quickly. Power seats, like power windows, are ruggedly built and not likely to fail; but if yours do, they can be restored with replacement parts.

Whatever it is — instruments, doors, mirrors, handles, knobs, bulbs — they are all replaceable with duplicates, or if the car is elderly, with equivalent apparatus. You don't have to buy a new car because an ashtray knob is missing.

The Pleasure Dome on Wheels. The maintenance chores considered here, like those mechanical ones considered elsewhere, are easier to ignore than to perform.

Unlike the others, these can be ignored at no cost to the efficient running of the machine. But automobiles are important in our daily lives, and to many of us it is important that our automobiles give us positive pleasure, and that we avoid as far as possible the exasperation and depression that a shabby car engenders.

An automobile can be a pleasure whatever its age if you want it to be. If you maintain it in good condition, and if you are mindful of the alternatives, it can be even more of a pleasure at age 15 than at age 5.

10. THE MAINTENANCE SCHEDULES

The eight lists on the following pages are the heart of a preventive maintenance program. They are organized according to the intervals at which the inspections, repairs, and replacements should be carried out: some at 5,000-mile intervals, others every 10,000 miles, still others at intervals of 15,000, 25,000, 30,000, 50,000, 75,000, and 100,000 miles. If you drive your car about as much as the average car owner — 10,000 to 12,000 miles per year — this means you will have to schedule a session with your mechanic slightly more often than twice a year to have these operations performed.

There are five items in addition to those in the maintenance schedules that you should have done once a month at a gasoline stop (at a cost of about 15 minutes), and a sixth thing you should do by flicking a switch. These are listed on page 76.

These maintenance schedules will disagree with the owner's manual that came with your present car, and in some particulars the disagreement may be profound. Most of the discrepancies will reflect different judgments as to the economics of lubrication vs. replacement (this is discussed below), but some of them may be safety-related. It is a simple matter to compare inspection and lubrication schedules in your owner's manual (if they appear) for wheel bearings, steering linkages, brakes, and the exhaust system with our recommendations, and consult your mechanic about any point in which our recommendations appear to be less demanding than the owner's manual. Also, if your owner's manual prescribes maintenance operations for emission-control devices that do not appear in this book, or if recommendations disagree markedly, you should either follow the owner's manual or at least consult your mechanic. (It is almost impossible to cover the emission-control front in a book of this kind, so variegated are the devices in use in different makes and models of automobile. The situation will ultimately settle down, but probably not for several years, and it may become more complex before it becomes simpler.)

If you have two or three cars of different makes and covering a considerable range of model years, you will probably also find disagreement among the manuals for these automobiles. All this may make you wonder whether any maintenance schedule can be relied upon. It is a reasonable question, and in order to answer it, you need to consider the several factors that bear on the situation.

First of all: the most important consideration in good car maintenance is not the precise mileage at which you lubricate a joint, say, but rather the fact that you actually do lubricate it, and everything else, on some regular schedule. Your car's greatest enemy is its owner's tendency to Put It Off.

Secondly, almost every maintenance operation offers a trade-off between the cost of lubricating and the cost of replacement. That is to say, you can prolong the life of a joint in the steering system by having it lubricated very frequently, but if you overdo this preventive operation, the expenditures on lubrication will be higher than the cost of replacing the part more frequently.

Thirdly, any maintenance schedule proposed for general use may not fit a specific case. The automobile that is used almost exclusively for trips to the shopping center five miles away three times a week needs different maintenance in some respects from the car that takes its owner to work 50 miles from home every day on a superhighway. For this reason, some people may want to rewrite this maintenance schedule; if your car is in some kind of unusual service, you and your mechanic may find that some items need to be shifted around.

And fourthly, when you are reading the owner's manual that came with your car, remember that it reflects not only the wisdom of the engineers, but also the sales pitches of the salesmen. Generally speaking, the moving parts and the joints of any automobile are substantially identical with their counterparts in any other automobile of similar vintage, and they require substantially identical servicing in order to last a given length of time. But if one company embarks on a sales campaign that stresses "easy maintenance" — chassis lubrication only every 36,000 miles, for example — all the other companies have to respond somehow: either by claiming to be as "easy-care" as Brand X, or by stressing the "quality maintenance" offered by authorized dealers. In any case, you can't necessarily trust what you read in owner's manuals.

If you start this program with a new automobile, you can begin with your odometer at zero, and your first major session will come when the odemeter reads 5,000 miles. You will then ask your mechanic to perform all the operations on Maintenance Schedule A.

If you start the program with your present car, which already has 40,000 miles on it, say, or a used car you have just bought about which you know very little, your first actions will have to be somewhat more comprehensive. A sensible way to begin would be to read through all the maintenance schedules up to 40,000 miles, or whatever your mileage is. For 40,000 miles, this would be Schedules A, B, C, D, and E. Then you should have your mechanic carry out all the inspections, repairs, and replacements in these lists, unless you know for sure that they have already been done.

If you have owned the car since it was new, and if you keep records, you will know what has been done and when: "Replaced radiator hoses — 23,450," for instance. You may remember that kind of replacement even if you don't keep records because it happened in the middle of vacation, 2,000 miles from home, with the whole family, hot and irritable, watching and listening and perhaps commenting.

The chances are, however, that you don't keep records, and you don't remember. In that condition of doubt, the sensible course is to go through the schedules and have everything done, even if you lose a few miles here and there. The cost in dollars is small compared with the cost of breaking down and having to be towed in, and the benefit in peace of mind is great.

After you have got your car into good condition as a result of this overdue maintenance, then you can start at the 40,000 mark, or wherever, and continue from there into the indefinite future.

You may find yourself hesitating to take a list of things to do when you take your car to the garage. Always before, you have told your mechanic just to do what needed to be done, and now here you are armed with a list, or maybe even a whole book. Will he think you're crazy? Will he think you're a trouble-maker? Are you telling him to do something he already does routinely? Will he get mad, and take it out on you and your car?

A mechanic should welcome specific authorization to do things that will keep a car in good condition and that he will get paid for doing. A mechanic, however, is as human as the rest of us and he may react to your sudden interest in his work by resisting it, or even resenting what he thinks of as meddling.

The only sensible way to approach this problem is

by being open and good-humored. You are tired of being ignorant, you could tell him, and so you've decided to learn something about it. If he disagrees with anything you ask him to do, he should feel free to challenge it. He is, after all, the expert.

"Here's the list of things I'd like you to do," you can say. "Maybe you already do them all. And maybe you think it's not time to do some of them. But will you look it over, and tell me what you think?"

You may have to explain here that you are interested in keeping your car in the best possible condition for the longest possible time. Once he understands that basic fact, the rest will be easier.

So feel your way along. Go easy on his time, of course — he almost certainly has more business to attend to than he has time for — but while you're establishing a solid relationship with him that will last, if you're lucky, for years, don't worry about the fifteen minutes you're taking of his time right now. And if he's the kind of mechanic you want, together you'll establish a rapport that will make these maintenance lists the most important factor in the long life of your car.

These eight maintenance schedules include a total of 51 items. They cover the whole range from very simple and inexpensive to sizable and not at all inexpensive, from seemingly inconsequential items that are often neglected because they are not remembered, to items that are often neglected because they "cost more than I want to spend on an old car."

This last group includes the ones that may lead you to your new-car dealer's showroom; there is no escaping the fact that to have your car kept in satisfactory condition exacts its price in time and trouble — and money. And each of us indulges in a dream now and then of what life would be like if we could have transportation that was cheap and trouble-free and that demanded nothing of us. Your present car doesn't fit this description; a message of this book is that neither does a new car. Or any car.

Six Things To Check Regularly

It will take you fifteen minutes a month, at most.

Shortly before or soon after the first of every month, when you stop for gasoline:

1. Check the engine oil level. Most engines "use oil" (see page 134). Even if yours never needs oil between changes, it is sensible to have it checked once a month to be sure the situation is not worsening. If you are putting in as much as a quart each month, you should check it every time you get gasoline, or perhaps every second time.

2. Check the coolant level. This level may drop as a result of evaporation. If the level is too low, the engine will overheat, with results that can be serious. (See page 162.)

3. Check the battery electrolyte level. This level also drops as a result of evaporation. If you operate the car for a prolonged period with the electrolyte level too low, the battery will be damaged (page 173).

4. Check the level of the power steering fluid. If this level drops too low, the power steering pump may be damaged. (See page 220.)

5. Check the tire pressures, including the spare. If the tires are not sufficiently inflated, they will wear more rapidly than necessary. Also, under-inflated tires are dangerous at highway speeds. (See page 214.)

6. Run the air-conditioner at maximum setting for five minutes. This should be done in winter as well as in summer, so that the refrigerant/oil mixture will circulate. (See page 226.)

MAINTENANCE SCHEDULE A. Every 5,000 miles.

List for your mechanic:

Change oil and filter (but see item 2, below)

Chassis lube (but see item 3 below)

Check
   brake and transmission-cooler lines (but see
      item 4, below)
   front tires for abnormal wear
   manifold heat valve
   all fluid levels, including air-conditioner refri-
      gerant
   distributor-point resistance and dwell angle
      (but see item 8, below)
   all belts and hoses
   coolant freezing and boiling points
   battery condition

Oil transmission/clutch linkages, hood latch,
   and hinges on doors, tail-gate, and
   hood.

*For your own information, if you want to know
what you are talking about:*

1. Change the oil. The oil that has been circulating
through the engine has become contaminated with dirt,
grit, water, gasoline, and sludge. Fresh oil lubricates better. (See page 135.)

2. Change the oil filter every 5,000 miles if your car
is a 1967 model or older. More recent models can go
10,000 miles between changes. (See page 136.) The filter
strains out the dirt and sludge from the oil, and eventually
becomes clogged and ineffective.

3. Chassis lube. This refers to the lubrication of the
ball joints and other hinged joints in the suspension system (see page 208) and the steering system (see page
218), and also the universal joints (page 199) if they can

be lubricated. Lubrication reduces wear and postpones replacement. **Special note:** If the car is new, or if the ball joints have just been replaced, you can safely ignore them for 25,000 miles. After that, lubrication every 5,000 miles is advisable.

4. Brake and transmission-cooler lines and hoses should be inspected for leaks, rust, and rock damage each time the car is hoisted up for an oil change. The brake lines deliver hydraulic fluid to each wheel (see page 203), and the transmission-cooler lines (on automatic-transmission cars only, not manual-transmission cars) conduct transmission fluid (see item 7, below) to the radiator, up front, where it is cooled.

5. Inspect front tires for abnormal wear. The cause of the abnormal wear should be corrected to avoid premature wearing-out of tires. Front-end alignment (page 215) and worn-out front shock absorbers (page 211) are two likely causes.

6. Manifold heat valve should be checked for freedom of movement, and lubricated if necessary. This valve diverts hot exhaust gas to the carburetor when the engine is cold, to help the engine warm up (see page 153).

7. Fluid levels. This includes the differential oil (page 200), the manual-transmission oil (page 196), or automatic-transmission fluid (page 197), and the brake fluid (page 202). It also includes the power-steering fluid (page 220), if you have power steering, and the refrigerant level (page 226), if you have air-conditioning. Full charges of these fluids are essential for safe operation (or in the case of air-conditioning, for satisfactory operation), and any leaks should be noted and repaired promptly.

8. Distributor points. Cars that have electronic ignition do not have distributor points (see page 180), but in all others the distributor points are the vitals of the ignition system. They open and close several thousand times a minute; they must permit electric current to flow freely when they are closed (point resistance), and stay

closed (dwell angle) long enough to do their job, but not too long. (See page 180.)

9. Belts and hoses. Radiator and heater hoses should be checked for leakage and deterioration; failure of these hoses will shut you down (page 163). Gasoline hoses should also be checked; leakage here can be a fire hazard. Generator and water-pump belts are equally crucial (page 171). Other belts drive the power-steering pump (page 220), one kind of pollution-control device (page 153), and the air-conditioner (page 226).

10. Coolant. The ethylene glycol content of the coolant mixture must be high enough to prevent freezing in winter and boiling over in hot weather (page 161).

11. Battery condition. The liquid in each of the six cells is tested for sulfuric acid content. This is a measure of the state of charge of the battery (page 173). A seriously undercharged battery is not able to drive the starter.

12. Lubricate linkages and hinges. This reduces wear and postpones replacement. It also cuts down on noise and irritation and the resulting feeling that your car has served its time.

MAINTENANCE SCHEDULE B. Every 10,000 miles.

List for your mechanic:

Items on Maintenance schedule A (page 77),
    plus the following:

Change the oil filter (but see item 13, below)

Check the air filter

Re-gap the spark plugs

Clean the battery posts

Check the brake linings (but see item 17, below)

Under-side safety check: engine mounts, steering
    linkages and suspension joints (for
    looseness); and frame (for rust).

For your own information, this is what these items mean:

13. Change the oil filter. If your car is a 1967 or older model, this item belongs on List A, to be carried out every 5,000 miles. If it is newer, the item belongs here, to be attended to every 10,000 miles. The filter needs changing because in performing its job of straining out the dirt and sludge in the oil it becomes clogged and no longer works (page 132).

14. Check the air filter. A clogged air filter increases gasoline consumption (page 142). If it is the kind of filter that can be cleaned, it should be cleaned at 10,000 miles; if it is not, it should be replaced.

15. Re-gap the spark plugs. Each spark that jumps the gap causes a minute amount of metal to be lost by oxidation, and so the spark gap grows wider and wider. When the gap becomes too wide, the engine runs unsteadily and inefficiently (page 183). Spark plug manufacturers have persuaded the public that spark plugs must be *replaced* every 10,000 miles; and they have persuaded garage and filling-station people that it really is less expensive to replace plugs than to *clean and re-gap*

them. This is standard obfuscation. Indeed, *cleaning* a spark plug is a futile exercise, accomplishing virtually nothing (page 183) and not worth a mechanic's labor rates. But *re-gapping* — which is simply removing the plug, adjusting the gap, and putting it back again — is cheaper than buying a new one and paying for the labor of putting it in.

You may have some trouble with Reliable Old Bert on this one, not simply because R.O. Bert is looking at his profit on eight spark plugs at $1.50 each, but also because he has been reading the ads. "Let's give it a try," you can say to him; he'll shrug and give it a try.

16. Clean the battery posts. The battery posts accumulate a kind of corrosion that impedes the flow of current and makes the battery act as though it is weak, or even dead (see page 175).

17. Check the brake linings. Brake linings need no attention for their first 20,000 miles of city driving, or 30,000 miles of country or turnpike driving, so this item can be omitted if your car is new or if the linings have been recently replaced. In deciding whether or not to include it on your list, however, remember that front linings are usually replaced more frequently than rear linings (see page 204).

18. Under-side safety check: engine mounts, steering linkages and suspension joints, and frame. This general under-side inspection is not needed for the first 50,000 miles when the car is new, but it should be made at 10,000-mile intervals thereafter both as a safety precaution and to detect loosening of joints and linkages that make the car ride and handle like an old car (see pages 211 and 218). Engine mounts may in some cars permit the engine to get badly out of position if they fail; and the frame of the car may suffer rust damage from road salt or other corrosive influences (page 210).

MAINTENANCE SCHEDULE C. Every 15,000 miles.

List for your mechanic:

Items on Maintenance Schedule A (page 77) plus
        the following:

Replace distributor points, condenser, rotor (but
        see item 19, below)

Check timing

Check PCV system

Check front-end alignment

Clean or replace crankcase ventilation air filter

Inspect automatic choke

Check clutch-pedal travel (manual transmission)

Check emission-control devices (see item 26)

NOTE: Your car may have some of these listed
here, or all of them, or none, or it may have
others not listed here. In any case, this is the
time to have your emission-control devices inspected, whichever ones you have. Those discussed here are:
    air filter thermostatic control system
    spark advance control system
    thermal over-ride device for above system
    EGR system
    EFE system
    idle stop solenoid
    catalytic-converter protection system

For your own information:

    19. Replace the distributor points, the condenser,
and the rotor. These are crucial components of the
distributor (page 180) except in cars with electronic ignition (page 180). If you have such a car, do not include
this item on your list. Distributor points become pitted

and worn in service, and cause the engine to run unsteadily and inefficiently.

20. Check the timing. This term refers to the instant the spark occurs in the combustion chamber (page 184). It must be precisely accurate for best and most efficient engine operation. Engine wear causes timing to change gradually.

21. Check the PCV (Positive Crankcase Ventilation) valve. If this valve is clogged or the hose is plugged, the engine will run inefficiently and perhaps unsteadily, and the engine may appear to be using oil (page 134).

22. Check the front-end alignment. Road shocks and wear of the suspension joints cause the front wheels to stray from the correct alignment, and this causes excessive tire wear and other problems (page 215).

23. Clean or replace the crankcase ventilation air filter. A clogged filter causes the engine to run unsteadily and inefficiently (page 150). Some filters can be rinsed clear over and over again; filters of other designs are inexpensive and are replaced instead of being washed.

24. Inspect the automatic choke. The choke controls the "richness" of the air/gasoline vapor mixture that enters the cylinders (page 145). The automatic choke causes the mixture to be rich in gasoline when the engine is cold, and less rich when the engine is hot. The mechanism may gum up after prolonged service, and become unresponsive to temperature changes. One result would be difficulty in starting the engine; at the other extreme would be poor gasoline mileage.

25. Check the clutch-pedal travel. This applies only to manual transmission cars. Clutch wear causes the clutch pedal and linkage to get out of adjustment, and this in turn causes excessive wear of the clutch face (page 198).

26. Check the emission-control devices. Some of these may be:

a. The air filter thermostatic control system. A damper feeds heated air to the carburetor as required to keep the temperature of the air stream at about 100°F. If the system does not operate properly, the engine will not develop full power over the whole normal range of operating temperatures.

   b. The spark-advance control system. At one extreme, the malfunction of this device will cause your engine to overheat, be wasteful of gasoline, and be deficient in power and pep. At the other extreme, malfunction will cause the engine to generate nitrogen oxide pollutants at levels in excess of legal limits.

   c. The thermal over-ride device for the spark-advance control system, above. In bumper-to-bumper traffic on a hot day your engine may overheat, partially as a result of the spark-advance control system doing its job properly. The over-ride device negates the spark-advance control system if the engine begins to overheat.

   d. The exhaust-gas recirculation (EGR) system reduces combustion temperatures and nitrogen-oxide formation; malfunction may be wasteful of gasoline. The early fuel evaporation (EFE) system permits "lean" fuel mixture to be used and saves gasoline; malfunction can cause engine stalling during warm-up period. See page 148 for both items.

   e. Idle stop solenoid. The function of this device is to reduce the engine idling speed when you shut off the ignition, to prevent "dieseling" or "after-running" of the engine after you turn it off.

   f. The catalytic-converter protection system. This is a device to prevent the throttle from closing too tightly, and sucking too much gasoline into the air stream during deceleration. (An excessively rich fuel mixture yields excessive unburned fuel and carbon monoxide in the exhaust, which cause the catalyst to overheat.)

MAINTENANCE SCHEDULE D. Every 25,000 miles.

List for your mechanic:

Items on Maintenance Schedule A (page 77), plus the following:

Replace all belts, radiator and heater hoses, air filter, fuel filter, carbon canister filter (but see item 31, below), distributor cap, radiator cap, and antifreeze

Service automatic transmission

Check electronic ignition system (but see item 36, below)

Pack the front-wheel bearings (rear-wheel bearings, too, if your car has front-wheel drive, but see item 37, below)

For your own further information, this is what these items mean:

27. Replace all belts. The air conditioner will not provide refrigeration if the compressor drive-belt fails (page 226). The power-steering pump is driven by a belt; without it, steering requires a great deal of effort, so much that the situation may become dangerous (page 220). The belt that drives the fan, the water pump, and the alternator is essential to the running of your car; its failure will shut you down because the engine will overheat quickly (see page 165).

28. Replace radiator and heater hoses. A leak in any of these hoses will shut you down almost immediately because of engine overheating (page 163).

29. Replace carburetor air filter. A dirty air filter causes excessive suction in the carburetor, which in turn results in excessive fuel consumption and loss of power (page 142).

30. Replace fuel filter. A plugged-up fuel filter reduces gasoline flow to the carburetor with results ranging from uncertain operation of the engine to total shut-down (page 141).

31. Replace the carbon-canister filter. This item applies only if your car is equipped with an evaporation control system (ECS) among its emission-control devices (page 149). A plugged-up filter or canister will make the engine run uncertainly, or even shut it down as though you have run out of gas.

32. Replace the distributor cap. Because of the very high voltage it is exposed to, the distributor cap slowly deteriorates, and permits leakage of the ignition current. Result: the engine will run shakily, or not at all, particularly in damp weather (see page 181).

33. Replace the radiator cap. The cap slowly deteriorates in service, and permits leakage of water vapor from the cooling system (page 162).

34. Replace the antifreeze. The ethylene glycol antifreeze is continuously subjected to oxidation by air. Oxidation converts ethylene glycol to oxalic acid; and oxalic acid is corrosive to the cooling system (page 161).

35. Service the automatic transmission. Details of this servicing will depend upon the design of your particular transmission. In some cases, internal adjustments are required, and in all cases internal strainers or filters must be cleaned or replaced, and fluid must be replaced (page 197). Neglect will cause the transmission to fail.

36. Check the electronic ignition system, if you have one. This is to confirm that your ignition system generates spark-plug voltage at the level required to assure easy starting and efficient operation (page 180). This operation corresponds to item 19, above, required if your car has a standard breaker-point ignition system.

37. Pack the front-wheel bearings. "Pack" means to pack with grease after first cleaning out all earlier grease. Neglect will cause the wheel bearings to be damaged; and if neglect goes on for too long it could cause the loss of a wheel (see page 214). Grease retain-

ers (see page 215) should be replaced whenever wheel bearings are packed.

Special Note: Mechanics customarily perform this operation — and charge you for it — whenever they overhaul the front brakes. If the front wheel bearings are far from due for greasing when the front brakes are overhauled, tell the mechanic *not* to pack the bearings.

If your car has front-wheel drive, consult your owner's manual about the optimum lubrication system for the *rear*-wheel bearings (see page 215).

MAINTENANCE SCHEDULE E. Every 30,000 miles.

List for your mechanic:

Items on Maintenance Schedules A (page 77), B
(page 80), and C (page 82), plus the
following:

Replace the PCV valve

Check the parking brake

*For your own information, if you want to know what
you're asking:*

38. Replace the PCV valve. This valve is subjected
to continuous wear. If it becomes leaky it will cause the
engine to run unsteadily, and it may increase the consumption of gasoline or oil (page 149).

39. Check the travel of the parking brake pedal (or
handle, or lever). As brake linings wear, the pedal (or
handle, or lever) must be moved further to apply the
brakes, and ultimately it will not be able to apply the
brakes before it reaches the end of its travel. Periodic
adjustment is therefore required (page 201).

MAINTENANCE SCHEDULE F. Every 50,000 miles.

List for your mechanic:

Items on Maintenance Schedules A (page 77), B (page 80), and D (page 85), plus the following:

Replace spark plug leads (but see item 40)

Clean battery cable connection on starter and battery ground connection on engine

Service catalytic converter (but see item 42)

For your own information:

40. Replace spark plug leads if your car is older than a 1975 model; if not, consult with your mechanic before deciding. The insulation on these wires to the spark plugs deteriorates in service and permits the high-voltage current to by-pass the spark plugs. This results in uncertain starting in damp weather, or unsteady running of the engine, or both. Traditionally, spark plug leads have been replaced reasonably frequently as a preventive measure, but many recent-model cars require leads that cost half again, or even twice, as much as wires for older models. This may persuade you to put it off for a time (see page 182).

41. Clean battery cable connections on starter and engine. Dirt and rust interfere with the flow of current from the battery to the starter. Even the slightest resistance at the point where the battery cable is connected to the starter, or at the point where the other battery cable is grounded — i.e., bolted — to the engine will cause the starter to operate sluggishly, as though the battery has gone weak or the starter has gone bad. The connection to the engine is neglected by many mechanics, and many a starter has been replaced unnecessarily, when all that was needed was a good cleaning and tightening of the battery ground connection. See page 123.

42. Service the catalytic converter. The catalytic converter was first introduced in 1975-model cars. At the time of this writing it was expected to operate "for at least 50,000 miles" before it needed attention. Consult your mechanic as to what his experience will have shown to be needed. See page 155.

MAINTENANCE SCHEDULE G. Every 75,000 miles.

List for your mechanic:

Items on Maintenance Schedules A (page 77), C
      (page 82), and D (page 85), plus the
      following:

Replace the fuel pump

Replace the water pump and the thermostat

Replace the universal joints (but see item 45
      below)

Replace the shock absorbers

For your own further information:

43. Replace the fuel pump. When your fuel pump
fails, it shuts you down (see page 140). Many a fuel
pump has lasted more than 100,000 miles, but very
many more have not. Preventive replacement, furthermore, enables you to have a *new* fuel pump installed;
emergency replacements often must be rebuilt pumps,
which cost almost as much and are not likely to last as
long as new ones.

44. Replace the water pump and the thermostat.
While you can usually limp home on a leaky water
pump, it is worrisome, and a great deal of trouble to
travel very far (see page 165). The comments in item
43, above, apply equally to water pumps. Thermostat
replacement is included here because it increases the
cost of the job by only the price of the thermostat — a
few dollars at most — and because the thermostat does
not have an unlimited life expectancy (see page 166).

45. Replace the universal joints. Universal joints
usually warn you well in advance, by means of noise or
vibration, before they shut you down; but if they have
lasted for 75,000 miles it is safe to expect that they will
soon begin to cause vibration that will cause the car to

feel old (see page 199). Before definitely deciding to replace them, however, you should consult your mechanic; you may be able to defer the replacement for another ten or twenty thousand miles.

46. Replace shock absorbers. Shock absorbers in normal service have three to four times the life-expectancy that most of the public and many otherwise sensible mechanics assume (see page 211). The time will eventually come, however, when your shock absorbers should be replaced. You may be able to get more than 75,000 miles out of them, but by this time they are probably not doing their job as well as they used to, and you would probably be happier with the feel of the car if you replaced them.

MAINTENANCE SCHEDULE H. Every 100,000 miles.

List for your mechanic:

Items on Maintenance Schedules A (page 77), B (page 80), D (page 85), and F (page 89), plus the following:

Replace the alternator and the voltage regulator

Replace the carburetor

Replace the spark coil

Replace the ignition switch

Drain and refill the differential

For your own further information:

47. Replace the alternator and the voltage regulator. The alternator will ultimately fail to provide charging current for the battery, and you will not be able to travel very far before it shuts you down (page 171). Although the alternator might last a few tens of thousands of miles more before it fails, replacement at 100,000 miles is inexpensive insurance. The voltage regulator (page 171) is also subjected to wear and it too can cause failure of the charging system; replacement at a time you choose is much preferable to a time *it* chooses.

48. Replace carburetor. Internal wear of carburetor parts causes increased fuel consumption and deterioration in engine performance (page 142). A subnormal carburetor is not likely to shut you down, but savings in gasoline will pay for a new carburetor within a comparatively short time. *Do not install a rebuilt carburetor* (page 145).

49. Replace spark coil. If the spark coil fails, it will shut you down (page 179). The coil is likely to last longer than 100,000 miles, but as it deteriorates, it causes the engine to be more difficult to start, particularly in cold or damp weather.

50. Replace the ignition switch. The contact points

suffer a minute amount of spark damage each time the starter is operated (see page 121); hence the switch will not last forever. If most of your mileage is in short trips, the switch will deteriorate more rapidly than if long trips are the rule in your life. Replacing the switch at 100,000 is a good compromise.

51. Drain and refill the differential. Almost all owner's manuals suggest, if they do not actually state, that the grease in the differential will last forever and needs neither maintenance nor replacement. This is not exactly correct, because over a number of years that grease will probably thicken and become less effective as a lubricant. A refill every 100,000 miles is sensible.

11. SYMPTOMS

Any automobile, however new or however well-maintained or both, will now and then develop noises, odors, vibrations, and silences as a result of something not working properly. The most important thing about these manifestations is that *they are telling you something.* Therefore, *pay attention.*

The more common of these ailments are listed in the following pages, together with their probable causes. You will also find attached to each one — except where it is clearly unnecessary — an *urgency rating,* which tells you how important it is that you do something about it. (An example of the unnecessary: your car is shut down because the starter won't work; you don't need to be told how urgent a matter that is because you won't be moving at all until it's fixed.) The range is wide: a door rattle can continue indefinitely without harming anything except perhaps someone's peace of mind, but faulty brakes, or a precipitous drop in the oil pressure, or serious overheating of the engine with clouds of steam — such problems need attention NOW. Most fall somewhere between the two extremes.

The Urgency Scale

URGENCY 1: Have the problem investigated next time the car goes to the garage or service station for routine maintenance.

URGENCY 2: Have the problem investigated the next time you stop for gasoline.

URGENCY 3: Take the car in as soon as you can conveniently do so.

URGENCY 4: Take it in today or tomorrow even if it is inconvenient.

URGENCY 5: Stop at the side of the road immediately.

Starter won't operate: merely clicks, or not even that. In increasing order of complexity:

a. "Neutral" switch (automatic transmission) (page 122) or "clutch switch" (manual transmission) is out of adjustment, and so current can't flow.

b. The battery is undercharged (page 173).

c. Battery posts have become corroded (page 175), and so current can't flow to the starter.

d. Battery ground connection has become corroded (page 123).

e. The ignition switch has failed (page 121).

f. The solenoid switch (page 120) that operates the starter has failed.

g. The starter itself has failed (page 120).

h. The fusible link has blown (page 223).

Starter cranks slowly and with difficulty. URGENCY 4, since next time it may not crank at all.

a. The battery is undercharged (page 173).

b. Battery posts have become corroded and are impeding the heavy current the starter needs (page 175).

c. The battery ground connection has become corroded, with same effect as (b), above (page 124).

d. The starter solenoid switch contact points have become pitted and do not conduct current as freely as they should (page 120).

Starter operates (goes "ruh-ruh-ruh") but engine doesn't catch. In increasing order of complexity:

a. Out of gasoline.

b. Engine flooded by excessive pumping on accelerator pedal (page 146).

c. Wet distributor cap and/or spark plug cables (page 181 and 182).

d. Distributor points badly out of adjustment because of excessive wear (page 180).

e. Automatic choke needs adjusting (page 145).

f. The gasoline has water in it (page 140).

Beyond these comparatively trivial malfunctions lie many more complex ones in both the ignition system (page 178) and the fuel system (page 139).

Engine catches, but prolonged cranking needed. URGENCY 1 — 4, depending on how exasperating it is.

a. Engine is flooded because of excessive pumping on accelerator pedal (page 146).

b. Automatic choke needs adjusting (page 145).

c. Distributor points out of adjustment because of excessive wear (page 180).

d. Spark plugs are out of adjustment or need replacing (page 183).

More complex problems may exist in either the ignition system (page 178) or the fuel system (page 139).

Engine stalls repeatedly during warm-up period. URGENCY 1 — or perhaps 2 in some traffic conditions.

a. Engine idling speed has decreased too much because of wear of carburetor linkages (page 147).

b. Fuel mixture has got out of adjustment because of carburetor fouling (page 147).

c. Chilly, dank weather is causing ice to form in the

carburetor (page 143).

d. Unseasonable cold wave has caught the filling stations and you with summer-grade gasoline in wintry weather (page 144).

e. Distributor points have gone out of adjustment because of excessive wear (page 180).

Engine runs unsteadily; hesitates and jerks. URGENCY 2. This problem is not likely to shut you down, but if it has developed over the course of a few days or less, it may be a symptom of something failing that *could* shut you down. If it has merely progressed over a period of a week or two, however:

a. A spark plug lead may have failed (page 182).

b. The spark plug gaps may have become excessively wide in too-prolonged service, and need re-gapping (page 183).

c. The distributor points may have got out of adjustment as a result of excessive wear (page 180).

d. The automatic choke may be stuck in a closed or partly-closed position (page 145).

e. The air filter may be badly plugged (page 142).

f. The gasoline has water in it (page 140).

g. The PCV valve (page 149) or the crankcase ventilation filter (page 150) is plugged.

Engine expires: dies in mid-flight.

a. Out of gasoline.

b. Fuel filter badly plugged (page 141).

c. Fuel pump gone bad (page 140).

d. The carburetor has been fed a slug of water (page 140).

e. Distributor points badly out of adjustment as a result of excessive wear (page 180).

f. Ignition coil or condenser suddenly gone bad (page 179).

g. The fusible link has blown (page 223).

High-pitched buzz when engine is cold; disappears on warm-up. URGENCY 1. Minor malfunctioning of the manifold heat valve (page 153): it tries to stay shut when the engine is cold, but exhaust pulsations force it open, whereupon it closes again, audibly.

Squeal under the hood.

a. Slipping belt — as evidenced by occurring only when you race the engine (usually the alternator belt), or turn quickly to right or left (usually the power steering belt), or turn on the air-conditioner. URGENCY 2. Slipping increases wear on a belt, and thus enhances the chances of belt failure.

b. Low fluid level in the power steering unit — as evidenced by continuous squeal or howl when the engine is running. URGENCY 4. The pump will be damaged if it is run very long like this (page 220).

c. Water-pump seal is failing (page 165).

Engine "spits back" through the carburetor on acceleration. URGENCY 2.

a. Automatic choke may be out of adjustment (page 145).

b. Carburetor acceleration pump may be malfunctioning (page 146).

c. There may be electrical leakage from one spark plug lead to another, permitting the wrong spark plug to fire (page 182).

d. An intake valve may be leaky (page 129).

Oil consumption increases appreciably over a short period of time. URGENCY 2.

a. Leak in the engine lubrication system (page 134).

b. PCV valve plugged (page 149).

c. Leaky diaphragm in vacuum-windshield-wiper system (page 134).

Engine noises of various degrees of ominousness:

Light peck-peck-peck sound when the engine is cold, but goes away as the engine warms up. This is probably the valve tappets that need adjusting (page 130), or a hydraulic valve lifter not doing its job (page 129)—perhaps only temporarily—or a worn fuel-pump push rod (page 140). URGENCY 1.

Light clack-clack-clack sound—noisier than the peck-peck-peck described above, but not a heavy thudding that tells even a novice that there's real trouble afoot. Probably a hydraulic valve lifter gone inoperative (page 129), perhaps only temporarily because of a speck of dirt or carbon in the oil it lives on. However it could be something more serious. URGENCY 4.

Heavy thud-thud-thud. URGENCY 5. A main bearing or connecting rod bearing may have failed, or a piston may have broken. Any further operation, even brief, may cause serious additional engine damage.

Dead gauges. The fuel gauge, the water temperature gauge, and the oil-pressure gauge are protected in some but not all automobiles by a fuse. If all three, (or if you have only two of these three, both) go dead, suspect the fuse first. URGENCY 2. If you have only a fuel gauge and it goes dead, then the trouble may be either in the fuse or in the fuel-gauge assembly itself (page 139). URGENCY 2

"Hot" warning light doesn't go on when key is turned to "Start." URGENCY 4. This light is supposed to go on while the starter is operating, to prove that the bulb is not burned out. If it doesn't go on, that means the warning system is inoperative—so if the engine overheats (which could damage the engine) you won't even know it.

"Cold" warning light doesn't go on when the engine is cold. URGENCY 1 in summer, URGENCY 2 in winter. The engine won't suffer trauma if it operates at too low a temperature, but fuel economy will suffer and the oil will have a greater tendency to produce sludge (page 167).

Engine fails to warm up to normal operating temperature. URGENCY 1. If the engine operates at a temperature that is too low the result will be excessive fuel consumption and excessive sludge formation in the engine oil, but you can run several days or even several weeks without damage. The condition should not be allowed to persist for months, however.

a. The thermostat may be stuck in the open position (page 167).

b. It may be an instrument or warning-light-system problem and not an engine-temperature problem at all (page 167).

Engine overheats. URGENCY 1 if it is merely a problem of the temperature gauge indicating a slightly higher temperature than normal; URGENCY 5 if you have clouds of steam, or if the engine gives other evidence of overheating; URGENCY 2 to 4 for other problems.

a. Coolant level may be too low because of a liquid leak in the system or a vapor leak through the radiator cap (page 168). (Clouds of steam almost always mean a ruptured radiator or heater hose.)

b. The fan belt may have failed, which usually halts not only the fan but also the water pump, and as a result, the circulation of the coolant (page 165).

c. In summer: the concentration of ethylene glycol in the coolant may be too low, hence too much water has evaporated away, and the coolant level has dropped too far (page 161).

d. In winter: the concentration of ethylene glycol may be too low and the coolant may have frozen, hence it cannot circulate, and the liquid trapped in the coolant jacket is converted to steam (page 162).

e. The cooling system thermostat may have become inoperative in the closed position, thus impeding or preventing circulation of the coolant (page 166).

f. A too-heavy trailer load may be causing the engine to work above its rated capacity.

g. The temperature gauge or temperature alarm light may be giving a false signal (page 167) — that is, you don't have a cooling problem at all, but instead you have an instrument problem.

Cloud of steam up front. URGENCY 4. A radiator hose or heater hose has ruptured or become disconnected and is squirting coolant on the hot engine (page 163). The engine will soon overheat for want of coolant, but you can operate it cautiously until it does overheat, as indicated by the water temperature gauge or the alarm light (page 167). You may be able to limp to a service station; but shut the engine down as soon as you have evidence of overheating.

Leaks: water spots or puddles on the pavement or the garage floor.

a. Just forward of the right front door, after the air-conditioner has been running: merely means that your air-conditioner is operating properly, and squeezing water out of the humid air.

b. Underneath the engine or the radiator, either up front or at the rear. URGENCY 4. Something in the cooling system is leaking; and leaks in the cooling system cannot be tolerated for very long (page 168).

Leaks: oil spots or puddles on the pavement or the garage floor.

a. Up front, underneath or slightly behind the radiator. URGENCY 4, since it may be the transmission fluid leaking from the fluid-cooling section of the radiator.

b. Underneath the engine:

A pronounced leak that has developed slowly, URGENCY 4.

A minor drip underneath the engine: URGENCY 1. This normally means either leaky rocker-arm-cover gaskets (page 129), which are easy to repair or replace, or leaky oil seals around the crankshaft (page 134), which you won't want to have repaired unless the leak is pretty annoying.

An oil leak underneath the engine at the front end on the driver's side may also mean a leaky power-steering-pump seal (page 220), URGENCY 2; at the rear end of the engine on the driver's side, the spot may mean a leaky steering-box seal (page 236), URGENCY 1.

c. Amidships of the car: a pronounced leak that has developed suddenly is URGENCY 4. A leak here is usually from an oil or grease seal in the transmission (page 197).

d. At the rear of the car, between the rear wheels. URGENCY 1. The grease seal in the differential (page 200) may need replacing.

Oil-pressure warning light fails to light when you turn the ignition on. URGENCY 4. This means that the bulb or the sending unit (page 236) is not working — which means that your oil-pressure alarm system is not working. This is not important as long as the lubrication system is performing properly, but if it stops performing properly, you won't know, and the engine could be seriously damaged (page 131).

Oil-pressure warning light goes on (or stays on) when the engine is running. URGENCY 5, until you confirm that the oil level in the crankcase is above the danger mark; thereafter, URGENCY 4. The oil-pressure sending unit may have gone bad (see page 236). This in itself is serious only in that it knocks the warning system out of action, so you won't be warned if the engine lubrication system actually does fail, in which case the engine would be severely damaged. (See page 131.) Have the warning system repaired as soon as you can get somebody to work on it.

Oil-pressure gauge indicates unusually low pressure.

a. URGENCY 5, if the pressure drops to 5 pounds per square inch or less when the engine is running. Confirm that the crankcase oil level is above the danger mark, then URGENCY 4.

b. URGENCY 4 if the pressure drops below 10 pounds per square inch but stays above 5 psi when the engine is running.

In either case, drive sedately until you can have the

problem looked into. The second situation may be normal for your car when the engine is summer-hot and it is idling. In either case, the oil-pressure sending unit (page 236) may have gone bad. It is important, however, to establish that the engine lubrication system is working properly (page 131), and to make any repairs to the oil-pressure instrument that may be needed.

"Gen" (or "Alt" or "Bat") light fails to go on when you turn the ignition on before starting the engine. The bulb has probably burned out or worked loose in its socket. URGENCY 3. You have an alarm system that is inoperative, which is sometimes worse than no alarm system at all. The battery may run down without your knowing it (page 173).

"Gen" (or "Alt" or "Bat") light goes on, or "Charge" or "Battery" gauge indicates DISCHARGE at speeds above idling speed. URGENCY 4. The alternator or generator is not generating current at a high enough rate to keep the battery charged. Result: the battery will run down as you continue to operate the car, and will run down very rapidly if you draw heavy currents for headlights, heater motor, etc.

　　　a. The alternator or generator drive belt may be slipping or broken (page 171).

　　　b. The voltage regulator may have failed or may be out of adjustment (page 171).

　　　c. The alternator or generator may have gone bad (page 171).

Gasoline consumption soars. URGENCY 3.

　　　a. The automatic choke may not be opening completely when it should (page 145), causing the fuel mixture to be too rich.

　　　b. The air filter may be plugged, also causing fuel mixture to be too rich (page 142).

　　　c. The breaker points may be overdue for adjustment or replacement, resulting in incomplete fuel combustion (page 180).

　　　d. The spark plugs may be overdue for adjustment

or replacement, with the same result (page 183).

Gasoline odor in the passenger compartment.
a. If this is apparent only after the car has been in a closed garage, and dissipates as soon as the car is operated, URGENCY 2. Check for a fuel-line leak (page 140).

b. If it is apparent after parking outside as well as inside, but goes away upon starting the engine, URGENCY 3 if odor is faint, URGENCY 4 if it is even moderately strong. The fuel pump or a fuel connection underneath the hood is leaking slightly, and there is some fire hazard.

c. Gasoline odor pronounced: URGENCY 5. The fuel pump or a fuel connection underneath the hood is leaking appreciably, and there is considerable fire hazard.

Exhaust odor in the passenger compartment. URGENCY 4 — and drive with windows open enough to sweep out the exhaust odor. Exhaust fumes in the passenger compartment are DANGEROUS.

a. The trunk lid may be open, and eddy currents are pulling exhaust fumes into the car via the trunk and the back seat.

b. A component of the exhaust system (page 152) may have developed a major leak.

Exhaust roar. The muffler or exhaust pipe or other part of the exhaust system needs replacing. URGENCY 3; and in the meantime drive with the windows open. Exhaust fumes seeping into the car can kill you. See WARNING, next page.

Hissing overtone to normal exhaust sound. URGENCY 3. This usually means that the tailpipe has been crimped or flattened at the end, restricting the flow of exhaust gas. Result: loss of power and excessive fuel consumption.

Smoky exhaust. URGENCY 1.

a. Black smoke, or soot stain on the pavement where the tailpipe directs the exhaust stream onto the pavement, means a too-rich fuel mixture. The automatic choke (page 145) may not be opening properly. The air filter may need replacing (page 142). Black smoke is evidence of high fuel consumption.

b. Blue smoke means that oil is getting into the combustion chamber.

    i. Piston rings may be coming to the end of the road (page 130).

    ii. The PCV valve may be plugged and causing crankcase pressure to be high enough to force oil up past the piston rings at an abnormally high rate (page 149).

Warning About Exhaust Systems

Leakage in the exhaust system will not shut down the car, but it may shut down the occupants. Exhaust gas contains a high concentration of carbon monoxide, which can kill you. Exhaust gas from a leak in the system can seep into the car, particularly when the car moves little but the engine continues to run, as in traffic jams or when stalled because of slippery roads. First symptoms are drowsiness and headache. IF YOU SMELL EXHAUST, OPEN THE WINDOWS NO MATTER HOW COLD OR WET OR UNPLEASANT IT IS OUTSIDE; and have the exhaust system checked promptly.
URGENCY 4.

Tail pipe scrapes on pavement at driveways. URGENCY 2.

a. A clamp or hanger on the muffler or the tailpipe has failed and permitted the tailpipe to drop to a lower position than is proper.

b. The rear springs have sagged (page 213).

Engine runs, but car won't move. The only trivial cause of this problem is that one wheel is on ice or in snow or mud so that it achieves no traction. All other possible causes lie deep in the drive train (page 191): a failed clutch, or transmission, or universal joint, or differential assembly, or rear axle.

Engine runs inordinately fast when in gear, compared with the speed of the car. URGENCY 3 with manual transmission, URGENCY 4 with automatic transmission. If the engine seems to race ahead while the car is reluctant to follow — the comparison is necessarily based on your feel for the car — it means that there is appreciable slippage in the clutch (manual transmission) or in the transmission itself (automatic transmission). In either case, drive sedately until you find out what the trouble is. The clutch may merely need adjusting (page 193), or the automatic transmission may merely need fluid (page 197) — unless you damage the ailing component by demanding too much of it in its temporarily weakened condition.

Metallic whine when the car is in motion. URGENCY 4.

a. A wheel bearing may have gone bad, or may need grease, or both (page 214).

b. A brake shoe may be rubbing against the rotating drum because of a broken return spring. (See Sketch 13, page 201).

The car vibrates or shudders when the clutch pedal is being let up. URGENCY 3. Drive conservatively until you find out what the trouble is, since harsh treatment might damage the clutch.

a. The clutch may need adjusting (page 193).

b. An engine mount may have come loose or failed, permitting the drive train to be distorted out of alignment or to wobble.

c. The clutch may need overhauling (page 198).

The car vibrates or shudders in reverse (automatic transmission). URGENCY 3. Drive slowly until you find out what the trouble is, since harsh treatment might damage the transmission. The most probable cause of the difficulty is loose or broken engine mounts, which result in mis-alignment of the drive train.

Vibration of the car at high speeds. URGENCY 3, or even 4, if the car also vibrates at low to moderate speeds; URGENCY 1 if the car is stable at those speeds.

    a. Tires may be out of balance (page 213).

    b. A pair of shock absorbers may need replacing (page 211).

    c. A universal joint (page 199) may need replacing.

Stick shift jumps out of gear or sticks in gear. URGENCY 3.

    a. The clutch may need adjusting (page 198).

    b. The transmission lubricant level may have dropped too low.

    c. Transmission parts may need replacing.

Rubbing noise when the clutch pedal is pushed in.

    a. If it occurs when the engine is stopped, URGENCY 1. It means that the clutch linkage is improperly lubricated, or worn, or out of adjustment, or the pedal itself has somehow got bent and is rubbing on the floor board.

    b. If it occurs when the engine is running, URGENCY 2. The clutch release bearing may need grease, and prolonged further operation may cause appreciable wear (page 195).

Gear clash when you shift gears. URGENCY 3.

    a. The clutch may need adjusting (page 198).

    b. The transmission lubricant may have leaked out, so that the lubricant level is too low.

    c. Gears or shafts in the transmission may need replacing.

The transmission whines or groans.

a. If the noise develops or becomes noticeably louder over a period of a few days or a few weeks, URGENCY 4, because it probably means that the transmission-lubricant level is seriously low.

b. If the noise has been with you for months, and is becoming louder only gradually, URGENCY 1, since it probably means that gears or shafts or both in the transmission have become worn.

CLUNK sound in the rear when you shift into "D" or "R" (automatic transmission). URGENCY 1, or URGENCY 2 if it irritates you.

a. The idling speed may be too high; normal slack in the drive train is taken up with a "whack" when shafts reverse direction quickly.

b. The level of the lubricant in the differential (page 200) may be too low.

c. A universal joint may need replacing (page 199).

A sharp metallic rattle or a clunk on bumps. URGENCY 4 if this has developed suddenly; URGENCY 1 — 3 if it has developed over a period of weeks or months.

a. A shock absorber mounting may have come loose (page 211).

b. An exhaust pipe or muffler mounting may have broken (page 156).

c. Front or rear suspension pivots may have become loose through wear (page 210) and need to be replaced.

d. Rear spring may have broken a leaf (page 208).

The car hits bottom on bumps. URGENCY 2 if the thump is in the rear; URGENCY 3 if it is in the front. The problem is almost certainly caused by worn-out shock absorbers, which should resist motion in both directions (page 211). Worn-out front shock absorbers cause abnormally rapid wear of front tires (page 212) and make it more difficult to control steering; faulty rear shock absorbers also make for sloppy control. In either case, the car bounces around instead of being stable, and this introduces some additional hazard to driving.

The brake pedal sinks almost to the floor. URGENCY 4 — and drive slowly and carefully in the meantime. The brake system on either the front wheels or the rear wheels has failed, so that you have only about half (or less) of your normal braking capability (page 203).

The brake pedal sinks all the way to the floor. URGENCY 5. But you can limp to home and mechanic by using your parking brake. But DRIVE SLOWLY AND CAREFULLY: the hydraulic brakes on all four wheels have failed and your parking brake is a *very poor substitute* for the foot brake (page 201).

The brake pedal travels abnormally far before the brakes work. If the condition has developed slowly, over a period of days or weeks, it probably means that the brakes need some adjusting. You can take care of this yourself by putting the car in reverse and applying the brakes a few times. This automatically adjusts the brakes. If the pedal travel does not shorten up perceptibly after this, then the problem is more serious. URGENCY 4, in that case, since it may mean a loss of brake fluid (page 202).

The brake pedal feels spongy. URGENCY 4 — and drive carefully on your way to the garage. Sponginess almost certainly means that air has been sucked into the hydraulic brake system; this air cushion interferes with the braking action. Also, air can be drawn in only if the brake fluid is leaking out. And if any brake fluid should be deposited on a brake lining, you will have to replace the linings not only on that wheel but on its companion (front or rear) as well (page 205).

Hard brake pedal — meaning that you have to push down unusually hard on the brake pedal to get any braking action.

a. Brake linings may be wet as a result of going through deep water. URGENCY 1. The problem will clear up after you have applied the brakes a few times; this will dry out the linings (page 205).

b. Non-power brakes: there may be an obstruction of some sort that interferes with the brake pedal. URGENCY 4. Drive carefully until you investigate.

c. Power brakes: the vacuum booster may not be working properly. URGENCY 4. (See page 205.) Drive cautiously until you find out what is the matter.

The power brake loses power immediately when the engine stalls. URGENCY 3. The power system (page 205) is supposed to continue to supply a vacuum assist for at least 45 seconds after the engine stops. If it does not, a check valve in the system may need attention.

The brake pedal pulsates when it is depressed slightly. URGENCY 1. One or more of the brake drums (page 201) may have worn out-of-round, or a brake disc may have worn unevenly. It should be checked, but it is not necessary to correct it until the next brake overhaul.

The brakes squeal or chatter. URGENCY 3.

a. Muddy water may have been splashed into the brake unit on one wheel or several, in which case the ordinary use of the brake will cure the problem.

b. The brake linings (page 204) may be near or at the end of the road.

c. If the brakes have been recently relined, the friction surfaces — linings and brake drums — may require some wearing in before they make smooth contact at moderate contact pressure, in which case ordinary use of the brake will cure the problem.

The car pulls to one side when you brake. URGENCY 4. Drive with great care until you find out what the trouble is.

a. One of the front tires may be soft.

b. One front brake but not the other may have got wet (page 205).

c. Brake fluid or grease may have leaked onto one brake shoe or caliper (page 204).

d. Brake linings may have worn out (page 204).

The brakes grab, meaning that they seem to want to put you through the windshield, even when you push on the brake pedal with moderate pressure.

a. Normal, if it happens only when the brakes are cold, and disappears after the first few minutes of driving. This is a matter of the clearance between the brake shoes and the braking surfaces, which increases under normal operating temperatures.

b. URGENCY 4, if the condition develops fairly rapidly. It probably means that grease or brake fluid has leaked onto one or more brake shoes, which causes uneven brake action and can be dangerous. If you have the problem checked promptly, it may be possible to clean the brake linings and not have to replace them (page 204).

The brakes drag, meaning that the car doesn't coast freely, but feels as though the brakes are partially on when they are not.

a. You may have failed to release the parking brake.

b. A brake-return spring may have broken, so that one brake shoe is actually dragging against a brake drum. (See Sketch 13, page 201). URGENCY 4, because that brake shoe is being subjected to abnormal wear, and also because it will tend to pull the car to one side, which can be dangerous. Drive carefully.

Hard steering. URGENCY 4.

a. Manual steering: the front tires may be under-inflated.

b. Manual steering: the steering-gear box may need grease (page 218).

c. Power steering: the pump belt may be broken or slipping (page 220).

d. Power steering: if the hard steering is combined with a hissing noise, the pump urgently needs more hydraulic fluid. Stop at the nearest service station for fluid; the pump can be seriously damaged if it is operated for long in that condition (page 220).

The car wanders across the road or darts to right or left.

a. If the behavior has developed suddenly, URGENCY 4, since it may mean a loose wheel bearing (page 214) or loose lug nuts, or the failure of some part of the steering gear (page 218) or the front suspension (page 209). Drive very carefully until you find out what the trouble is.

b. If the behavior has developed gradually, URGENCY 1 — 3, depending on how unstable the car is. Steering-gear components (page 218), front suspension components (page 209), or front shock absorbers (page 211), may need replacing.

Shimmy — shuddering from side to side, usually only at low speeds.

a. If the problem has developed suddenly, without prior hint, URGENCY 4: lug nuts or front wheel bearings (page 214) may have worked loose.

b. The front suspension may be out of alignment (page 215). URGENCY 3, both because of the hazard of driving an unstable car, and because of the excessive front-tire wear.

c. One of the joints in the steering system may have worn to the point where it permits excessive freedom of motion of individual parts (See Sketch 17, page 219).

Tires wear unevenly or squeal excessively.
URGENCY 2.

    a. The tires may be under-inflated.

    b. The front suspension may be out of alignment (page 215).

    c. A shock absorber may have failed, allowing wheel "tramp" (page 212).

    d. The tire that is wearing unevenly may be out of balance (page 213).

Acrid odor of overheated electrical equipment. SHUT ENGINE OFF; TURN LIGHTS OFF until you determine whether you have an emergency. Open the hood, then turn on the key and look carefully for smoke. If you see any, URGENCY 5.

    If you pass this test and see no smoke, turn on any lights you had on before, and look again for smoke. If any appears, then URGENCY 5, if you can't operate without those lights; URGENCY 4, or perhaps URGENCY 3, if you can get along without them.

    If no smoke appears, then the chances are that some component in the heating system or the air-conditioning system is in the process of failing. Urgency depends on how dependent you are on the heater or the air-conditioner or whatever it may turn out to be.

Individual bulbs don't light. URGENCY depends on which bulb it is and the circumstances.

    a. The bulb may be burned out.

    b. The bulb socket may need replacing.

    c. The bulb socket, or the housing it is in, may be insufficiently grounded because of rust (page 222).

A whole system of lights won't light. URGENCY depends on circumstances.

    a. A fuse may need replacing (page 222).

    b. The switch that operates the system of lights may not be operating properly.

Light bulbs don't last long. This usually means that the voltage regulator is permitting the alternator to generate an excessively high voltage (page 171). URGENCY 3, since some of the bulbs that may burn out are difficult to reach and are thus expensive to replace.

Brightness of headlights fluctuates rapidly and markedly at uniform engine speed. URGENCY 4. A short-circuit in the headlight system is activating the circuit breakers to protect the circuit (page 223).

Headlights brighten and dim as engine speed changes. URGENCY 1.
    a. The battery may need replacing; the voltage drops excessively when the alternator is not actually pouring energy into it (page 173).
    b. The voltage regulator may not be holding the voltage as steady as it should (page 171).

The turn-signal lights flash at the wrong speed. URGENCY 3.
    a. A bulb in the system may need replacing.
    b. The flasher unit may need replacing.

The heater fails to heat. URGENCY depends on how much you need your heater.
    a. The thermostat in the cooling system may have failed, permitting the coolant temperature to stay too low (page 166).
    b. The thermostat in the heater unit itself may not be admitting hot liquid to the heater (page 225).
    c. The heater hose may have collapsed, blocking passage of the hot liquid to the heater (page 164).
    d. The fan on the heater may not be working because of a blown fuse (page 222).

The air-conditioner fails to cool. URGENCY depends on how much you need it.
    a. The compressor belt may have broken or may be

slipping.

b. The refrigerant may have leaked out of the system (page 226).

c. The air-conditioner control system may have failed (page 226).

The windshield washer won't squirt. URGENCY depends on circumstances (page 224).

a. The washer solution may have been used up.

b. The jets at the windshield may be plugged.

c. In winter: the washer solution may have frozen.

d. The washer-solution hose may have become disconnected or may have failed.

e. The valves inside the pump itself may need replacing.

The horn won't operate. URGENCY 3.

a. The wire connector may have pulled loose from the horn relay or from the horn itself.

b. The horn may need adjusting.

c. The horn relay may need replacing.

The horn won't stop operating. The only immediate EMERGENCY cure is to disconnect the wire from the horn, which you can do without damaging anything because of the simple snap-on connections. Then, URGENCY 3.

a. The horn relay may have failed.

b. The horn button may have got jammed "on."

12. YOUR CAR

You don't need to know how a car works in order to have it well taken care of, but some people find that once they establish a relationship with a car — in some respects like a relationship with a person—they want to know more about it. This section is an introduction to the subject.

The descriptions and explanations here are simplified. We have not attempted to be complete or profound; rather, we have tried to include only enough in each description to indicate the general principle involved and to show a little about how it is applied in this case. We have probably missed this goal on both sides and included some descriptions that are too detailed and some that are too general and vague. For these mistakes in judgment, we apologize in advance. Our primary purpose has been to give enough information to interest the somewhat-interested readers, but not so much as to intimidate them.

You will not find here a description of everything in every make of automobile, or even everything in your own particular automobile. There are dozens of new

devices that appear on this car or that, and even on
standard models there are many complicated details that
we do not try to cover. The important ones on your car
will be mentioned — perhaps even described — in your
owner's manual, and in any case your mechanic will be
able to guide you in their maintenance.

It is unlikely that you will want — or be able — to
read this section from beginning to end. It is primarily for
reference and for browsing, to be used in connection
with the Maintenance Schedules, list of Symptoms, and
the Index.

If your interest in your car should grow to the point
where you are tempted to tackle some of the maintenance work yourself — millions of people succumb regularly to this temptation, and more power to them — you
should arm yourself with a more detailed manual than
this pretends to be. Your public library contains many
such books, and from the array there or in a bookstore
you can select one or several suited to your level of
interest and ambition. If you find the subject at all com-
pelling, then you should buy the shop manual for your
make and model of car. Shop manuals can ordinarily be
obtained for at least five years, and sometimes for as
long as ten years, after the model year. The parts department of any authorized dealer for your make of car
will either order a shop manual for you or tell you how
to order it for yourself.

THE STARTING SYSTEM

The starting system cranks the engine to make it start. The system consists of the *battery* and *battery cables,* the *starter* with a *solenoid switch* to turn it on and off, and also a *switch* operated by the ignition key. If the car has an automatic transmission, the system includes a *neutral safety switch* that prevents the starter from operating except when the transmission lever is in the "neutral" or the "park" position. Sketch 1 shows the arrangement of these components. Some manual-transmission cars have a *clutch interlock* which permits the starter to operate only when the clutch pedal is fully depressed.

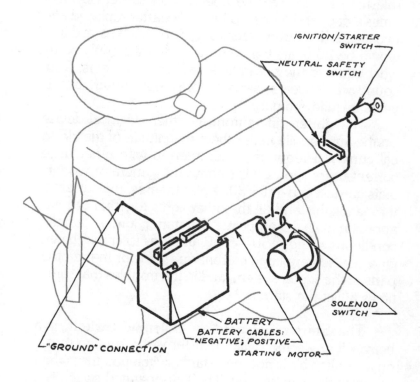

Sketch 1. Starting System

The **Starter** is sometimes called the **Starting Motor** or the **Cranking Motor.** (The latter term originated in the early days of the automobile when an engine could be started only by hand, using a crank.) The starter is a very powerful electric motor that might be suitable for use on a crane or a derrick, for lifting heavy loads. It rotates the flywheel and the other moving parts of the engine (see page 130 for descriptions of these), and enables the engine to start.

The starter itself does not require routine maintenance. Its life expectancy cannot be expressed in miles because mileage is not what wears it out: starting the engine is what wears it out, and the more often you start your engine, the sooner it will wear out. A door-to-door salesman reports that he operates his starter 50 or 60 times a day, and he has to have his starter replaced after two years. If you average, say, 5 or 6 starts a day, it would be 20 years before your starter accumulated the wear equal to the salesman's starter in two years. Don't count on 20 years' service from your starter, but 10 years is quite ordinary.

The starter differs from all other electrical devices on the automobile in the sheer magnitude of the electrical current it requires. A comparison with other major current-users shows this clearly: the generator working at its hardest generates 30 — 50 amperes; the current to the headlights and all the other lights together requires approximately 15 amperes; the starter, under ordinary conditions, needs 150 — 250 amperes to crank the engine. These very large currents are a factor in the other parts of the starter system, and in the troubles that sometimes afflict the starter.

The **Starter Solenoid,** or **Solenoid Switch,** is a heavy-duty electric switch that turns the starting motor on and off. This is *not* the "start" switch you turn when you turn the ignition key. The key-operated switch is a light-duty switch, as is (for example) the switch on a table lamp. The solenoid switch, on the other hand, is a very heavy-duty switch, as is (for example) the main switch that feeds current to an entire house.

The two switches work like this: when you turn the ignition key to "start," a current of about 40 amperes flows to the solenoid switch. This relatively small current causes the solenoid switch to slam shut, and a current of, say, 225 amperes then flows through the starting motor. The sketch on page 119 shows a solenoid switch in the main line from the battery to the starter, and an ignition/starter switch connected to the solenoid.

The solenoid switch does not require any routine maintenance. Like the starting motor, its life expectancy depends upon the number of starts rather than the number of miles, or number of elapsed months or years. Considerable sparking occurs each time the solenoid switch is closed to permit the heavy current to flow, and each time it is opened to halt the current; it is thus subject to a good deal of pitting and corrosion, called "burning." The solenoid switch is likely to have to be replaced sooner than the starter — after perhaps five, six, or seven years in ordinary service instead of ten. The solenoid switch will ordinarily give some warning by merely clicking when you turn the key to "start," rather than causing the starting motor to operate in its normal fashon. Be alert to such behavior. Ordinarily, after the solenoid has behaved that way the first time, the starter will operate the second or third time you try it. But this does not mean that the trouble has cured itself; it means that sometime soon the starter will *not* operate the second or third time you try it. Take it to your mechanic after the first or second warning.

The **Ignition Switch** is also part of the starting system. That is, when it is turned to "start," it activates the solenoid switch, which in turn allows current to flow to the starter. When the ignition switch is turned merely to "on," or turned to the left to operate the radio, of course it does not function as part of the starting system. It also functions as part of the ignition system. See page 178 for an explanation of this.

The ignition switch requires no routine maintenance, but its contact points suffer some sparking every time the starter is operated, like the solenoid switch, and it, too, is susceptible of failure after long service. The symptoms of approaching failure are the same as those described in connection with the solenoid switch: a click instead of the sound of the engine starting. When the car is taken in for an inspection of the solenoid switch, the ignition switch should be carefully checked also.

The ignition switch should be replaced as a precautionary measure every 100,000 miles.

How to Talk About Your Starter Problems

1. When you turn the ignition key to "start," and you hear nothing but a click, tell your mechanic "The solenoid just goes click; the starter isn't cranking the engine."

2. When the starter goes "rumrumrumrum," but the engine won't start, say "The starter is working but the engine doesn't start."

3. When you hear a loud clashing noise, as of steel against steel, when you operate the starter, say "I've got a starter gear clash."

The **Neutral Safety Switch,** or the **Clutch Interlock,** is intended to safeguard against starting the engine when the car is in gear. On cars with automatic transmission the safety switch permits the starter to operate only if the transmission is set in either "neutral" or "park." Not all cars with manual transmission have clutch-interlock switches, but on those that do, the switch permits the starter to operate only if the clutch pedal is fully depressed. (See page 193 for an explanation of clutch action and transmission gears.)

Both kinds of safety switches can get out of adjustment. If the starter won't operate, it may sometimes be induced to do so by moving the transmission lever slightly to the right or to the left of the "neutral" or the "park" position, or (in the case of a manual-transmission car) by letting up slightly on the clutch pedal. If the starter responds to such measures, it tells you the safety switch needs adjusting. This is a simple job, and you should have it done fairly promptly for two reasons: first, the switch may slip further out of adjustment and become entirely inoperative; and second, sparking occurs when you search out the proper position of shift lever or clutch pedal, and the switch points are not designed for such service.

Unless it has been operated for considerable periods when out of adjustment, the neutral safety switch or the clutch interlock switch is not likely to fail during the lifetime of the car, but since the safety switch is in the same circuit with the key-operated switch and the solenoid switch, it, too, is suspect when the other switches are under suspicion.

The **Battery** is discussed on page 173, in connection with the charging system.

Battery Cables, which are also discussed on page 175 in connection with the charging system, are important to the operation of the starter. Because of the magnitude of the current required by the starter, the battery cables are big, heavy wires. If they did not have to supply the starter they could be wires of much smaller size.

It is particularly important that all connections between the battery and the starter be clean and tight. The battery posts should be cleaned at regular intervals, as recommended on page 175. In addition and just as important, the battery cable connections at the ends away from the battery should also be detached, thoroughly cleaned, and replaced, every 50,000 miles. One of these cables goes to the solenoid; the other cable goes to

"ground." (See below for an explanation of this term.) If
your starter should become sluggish — if, for example, it
seems to labor excessively when you re-start the engine
when it is hot — one of the first things to suspect is a
corroded ground connection. In fact, corrosion at the
battery-cable connections can cause the starter to fail
entirely; even a small amount of electrical resistance at
any of these connections will reduce the voltage to the
starter to the point where it will not be capable of cranking the engine.

A sluggish starter should be attended to at your
next scheduled maintenance stop, or even sooner if the
sluggishness is pronounced. A starting motor draws very
large currents when it tries to crank an engine and inadequate voltage is supplied to it. Excessive currents
generate excessive heat in the starter, and excessive
heat causes damage and the damage is cumulative.

What "Ground" Means

Virtually all stationary electrical systems — in
homes and factories, for example — are
"grounded;" that is, they are connected at some
point to the ground, usually for reasons of safety.
Automobile electrical components are grounded by
connecting them to the frame of the automobile, or
to any metal object that is bolted directly to the
frame: the engine, the body, or metal parts inside
the body. In most automobile circuits, current flows
from the battery through a wire to a component;
the current then goes through the component,
doing whatever work it is required to do; it then
returns to the battery "through ground." Thus,
"ground" completes most electrical circuits in an
automobile.

Some automobiles with large engines have a
specific starter problem that baffles many mechanics:
when the engine is hot, as for example after going

through city traffic on a hot day, the starter is very sluggish or even entirely incapable of cranking the engine. In
some cases, at least, the problem can be solved by installing a new negative battery cable — the "ground" cable
— to connect the battery directly to the case of the
starter. Theoretically it should be adequate to ground
the battery to the engine block, but in some engines this
appears not to be adequate, after all. If you encounter
persistent starter problems of this kind, it will certainly be
worth while to try the direct-grounding treatment. If the
experiment works, the result is gratifying; if it doesn't, it
is not a very expensive failure.

Summary of Starting System Maintenance

Battery cable connections should be detached,
cleaned, and replaced every 50,000 miles. The ignition
switch should be replaced every 100,000 miles.
Otherwise, no routine maintenance is required.

THE ENGINE

The engine provides the power for the automobile. The basic power-generating operation, combustion, takes place here.

The engine consists of the *cylinder block (or engine block)*, the *cylinders*, the *cylinder head (or heads)*, the *pistons*, the *connecting rods*, the *crankshaft*, the *crankcase*, the *flywheel* and the *camshaft*. In addition, the engine contains a *lubricating system* that delivers oil under pressure to lubricate all its moving parts.

Several other systems, which are described separately under their own functions, are essential to the operation of the engine or to protect it from damage: the fuel system (page 139), the ignition system (page 178), the cooling system (page 160), and the exhaust system (page 152). Without these, the engine would be useless. Taken together, with the engine itself and its lubricating system, they comprise the power plant of the automobile.

The basic operating cycle of the automobile engine goes like this: a mixture of gasoline vapor and air is sucked into a cylinder through the intake manifold and the intake valve; the valve closes; a piston inside the cylinder moves upward and compresses the gasoline/air mixture; the compressed fuel mixture is then ignited by a spark from a spark plug; the fuel mixture expands explosively when it is ignited; the explosion pushes the piston and its connecting rod downward; this moves the crankshaft, which turns the flywheel. Think of your foot and leg pushing down on the pedal of a bicycle; it is the same kind of motion. At the same time, the exhaust valve opens and allows the burned gases to escape through the exhaust manifold; the piston moves upward again; the exhaust valve closes. This completes the cycle. The intake valve opens as the piston starts down again, and the cycle is repeated. Sketch 2 illustrates this basic operation.

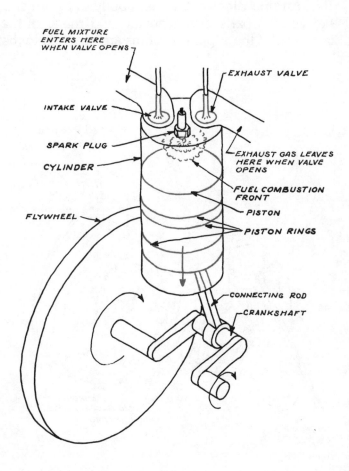

FUEL MIXTURE
ENTERS HERE
WHEN VALVE OPENS

EXHAUST VALVE

INTAKE VALVE

SPARK PLUG

EXHAUST GAS LEAVES
HERE WHEN VALVE
OPENS

CYLINDER

FUEL COMBUSTION
FRONT

FLYWHEEL

PISTON

PISTON RINGS

CONNECTING ROD

CRANKSHAFT

Sketch 2. The Basic Operation

An automobile engine has several cylinders and pistons, usually four or six or eight, depending on the design, and each one applies downward force on the crankshaft. Sketch 3 shows the location of cylinders (shaded lines), pistons, crankshaft, and flywheel inside an engine. Since the pistons fire in sequence, one after the other, very rapidly, the crankshaft is always being turned by one or another of the pistons.

   The **Engine Block** is the main body of the engine.
All the working parts of the engine and many of the
working parts of the support systems are attached to the
block.

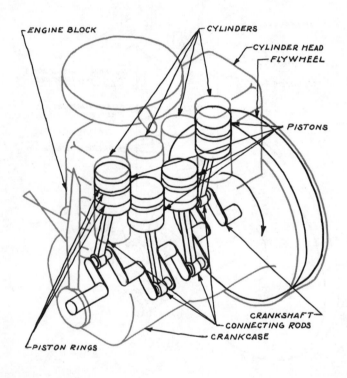

*Sketch 3. Location of cylinders, pistons, crankshaft and
flywheel in an engine*

   A **Cylinder** in an automobile engine is a cylindrical
hole bored through the engine block. In four- and six-
cylinder engines, the holes are almost always bored in a
longitudinal row; in an eight-cylinder engine, the cylinders are in two rows of four each, oriented in the form of
a V so as to point at a common crankshaft: hence the
term "V-8." Sketch 3 shows the location of cylinders
(portrayed by means of shaded lines) inside the engine.

The **Cylinder Head** is a slab of metal that is bolted onto the top of the engine block to provide caps for the cylinders. A V-8 engine has two cylinder heads, one for each bank of four cylinders. The cylinder head always contains threaded holes into which the spark plugs are screwed, and it usually contains the intake and exhaust valves as well. The cylinder head is labeled in Sketch 3.

Engine Valves are flat disks with beveled circumferences and vertical central stems, like mushrooms. Valves are included among the basic parts of an engine shown in Sketch 2; they are shown in greater detail, in connection with a discussion of valves in general, in Sketch 21 on page 239. Engine valves fit into beveled circular holes ("valve ports") in the cylinder head when they are closed, and are pushed clear of the holes when they are open, allowing the gasoline/air fuel mixture, or the exhaust gas mixture, as the case may be, to flow through. Heavy valve springs cause the valves to close; they are caused to open in the proper sequence by the valve gear, an assembly of cams, pushrods, and rocker arms. Sketch 21 also illustrates this. Part of the valve gear is attached to the upper side of the cylinder head; a valve cover made of sheet steel covers the valve gear, to keep lubricant in and dirt and water out.

The **Camshaft** is a longitudinal bar deep in the engine that is driven by the crankshaft. The camshaft is fitted with cams, or off-center lobes, which cause the pushrods to rise and fall. A sketch on page 231 shows this. The pushrods, in turn, push the intake valves and the exhaust valves open, and then permit them to close. These pushrods, and also the rocker arms, suffer as a result of this activity, and when they wear they become noisy; it is essential that the valve gear be adjustable to compensate for this wear. **Hydraulic Valve Lifters** are included in the valve gear of most American cars; they automatically and continuously make the needed adjustments to compensate for pushrod wear and thus avoid valve noise. If hydraulic valve lifters are not included in the system, then the pushrods have adjustable ends that are called **Valve Tappets.** These can be adjusted whenever valve noise becomes excessive.

Pistons are plugs that travel up and down inside the cylinders. They are similar in shape to an inverted open one-pound coffee can, and of roughly the same diameter but about half the height.

Piston Rings are spring-steel narrow rings that are mounted in grooves around the pistons. They press against the cylinder walls to seal against leakage around the pistons, to prevent loss of pressure following combustion. There are usually three rings on each piston.

Connecting Rods are links between the pistons and the crankshaft. A wrist pin attaches the connecting rod to the piston; this is a horizontal rod that goes through the piston from side to side, and through a hole in the upper end of the connecting rod.

The **Crankshaft** is a heavy steel shaft at the base of the engine that is turned by the downward thrust of the pistons and connecting rods acting rapidly and in sequence. This turning motion is transmitted to the **Drive Train** (see page 191) which ultimately turns the wheels and moves the automobile. Each crank on the crankshaft accommodates one connecting rod, except in a V-8 engine, where each crank is connected to a pair of cylinders.

The **Flywheel** is a heavy steel disk mounted at the rear of the crankshaft. It provides momentum and thus assures smooth rotation of the crankshaft. It also serves as the connecting link between the engine and the drive train. See page 191 for the section on the drive train.

The **Intake Manifold** is a heavy steel assembly with

ducts branching from it that is bolted onto the top or the side of the engine block to provide passageways for the fuel mixture to reach the intake valves. The passageways all come together at the top of the manifold, and the carburetor is bolted to it at that point. The significance of this is explained in the section on the **Fuel System,** beginning on page 139. It is shown in Sketch 4 on page 139.

The **Exhaust Manifold** is a similar heavy steel duct assembly that is bolted onto the side of the engine or cylinder head to provide passageways for exhaust gases to be conducted away from the exhaust valves. The passageways come together in a common duct onto which the exhaust pipe is bolted. The section dealing with the **Exhaust System** begins on page 152, and the location of the exhaust manifold is shown in Sketch 6 on page 152.

The **Engine Lubrication System** consists of an oil reservoir, called the crankcase, an oil pump, an oil filter, and an elaborate system of ducts and passages to all of the moving parts of the engine. The function of the engine lubricating system is to keep all of the moving parts of the engine bathed in oil or oil mist at all times when the engine is running. It must not fail in this function; if oil were not delivered to the moving parts in adequate quantity, it would be only a few minutes before the engine either labored to a halt or produced heavy thudding sounds that would betoken serious trouble to even an inexperienced ear.

The **Crankcase** is the lower half of the engine (see Sketch 3); it encloses the crankshaft, camshaft, and oil pump, and serves as the oil reservoir for the engine. The bottom of the crankcase is called the oil pan.

The **Dipstick** is the steel rod or strip with a ring or hook at the top that projects downward through a hole at the base of the engine into the crankcase. It is used for measuring the depth of the oil in the crankcase.

The **Oil Pump** is a simple pump located in the crankcase. Driven by the crankshaft or the camshaft, it sucks up oil from the crankcase, and pumps it through the lubricating system. When the engine is operating at ordinary driving speed, the oil pressure in the system in most engines is in the range 20 — 40 pounds per square inch — in the normal range of household water pressure. When the engine is idling and hot, the pressure may drop as low as 5 — 10 pounds per square inch.

The **Oil Filter** is a strainer, located outside the crankcase where it is easily accessible. The oil travels from the oil pump through the filter before going on to the moving parts. The function of the filter is to strain out of the oil all the dirt, sludge, gums, etc., that would aggravate wear of the moving parts. The oil filter is provided with a filter by-pass that permits the oil to bypass the filter if it should become clogged with the impurities it captures. The reason for this is that although feeding unfiltered oil to the moving parts may cause unnecessary wear, cutting off the flow of oil entirely, because of a clogged filter, would be disastrous.

Oil Passages lead to all the moving parts of the engine and through many of them, to supply oil to surfaces that cannot otherwise be reached. Thus, for example, the crankshaft is drilled with holes that receive oil from bearings in which the shaft rotates. This permits the oil to go to the connecting rods; the connecting rods are drilled with holes that conduct the oil on to the wrist pins; and the holes in the wrist pins conduct oil on to the cylinder walls. The oil is under pressure, and so it squirts from all the joints and bearings and is whipped into a mist by the moving parts. It ultimately falls back into the reservoir of oil in the crankcase, where it is picked up by the oil pump and returned to the engine — and so on, around and around.

The **Oil Pressure Indicator Light** or **Oil Pressure Gauge** is the most important item on your instrument panel because it notifies you if the oil pressure drops to a dangerous level. If you have an oil gauge, develop the habit of glancing at it regularly whenever the engine is running, including when it is idling. At moderate or high speeds, the hand of the gauge normally points somewhere in the range 10 o'clock to 1 o'clock, depending on the temperature of the engine (the hotter the engine, the lower the oil pressure); at idling speeds, even when the engine is hot, the hand must be well away from the lower end of the scale. Experience will teach you what is "normal" at idling speeds.

If you have an **Indicator Light,** it will go on when your oil pressure drops to a dangerous level. It is essential that you develop the habit of glancing at the light when you turn on the ignition, before you turn the key to "start," to check on whether the light is working. It is *intended* to go on at that time briefly, to provide you with information about the condition of the light itself. If it does *not* go on at this time, it means that the bulb has burned out or that the warning system has failed in some way. It is important to have the bulb replaced, or the system repaired, immediately; an alarm system that is inoperative is worse than useless — it is dangerous.

THE ENGINE MUST BE SHUT DOWN IMMEDIATELY IF THE OIL PRESSURE GAUGE READING DROPS ABNORMALLY, OR IF THE OIL WARNING LIGHT GOES ON.

The oil pressure warning system, whether gauge or indicator light, may itself be faulty, and so the warning may be a false alarm. If a warning is given, the oil level should be checked; if the oil level is within a quart (or in the case of a large engine, a quart and a half) of the full mark, then it would be safe to drive cautiously— watching engine temperature or temperature-warning light carefully, and listening carefully for any abnormal engine noises — to the nearest garage or filling station. It is a comparatively simple matter to determine whether the warning system itself is faulty. If it is, you may proceed normally, bearing in mind that you will not be warned if the oil pressure really does fail. The warning system should be repaired as promptly as possible.

If the warning system is found to be working properly, the engine should not be run further until the cause of the low oil pressure is determined.

Oil Consumption is a popular but often-erroneous measure of engine condition. If the piston rings don't do their job, then they do not wipe oil from the cylinder walls when the piston goes down; the result is that an excessive amount of oil is burned in the cylinders, along with the fuel mixture. But this is not the only route by which oil may escape from the system. It may simply leak out around oil seals where the crankshaft goes through the front wall or the rear wall of the crankcase, or under or through a gasket that is supposed to (but sometimes doesn't) make an oil-tight seal between the engine and some component that is bolted onto the engine. A plugged-up PCV (positive crankcase ventilation system — see page 149) can cause the air pressure inside the crankcase to be excessive, and this pressure may force oil past the crankshaft oil seals, or past the piston rings, or under or through gaskets that would not leak at normal pressures. And finally, if the car is equipped with a vacuum-powered windshield wiper, a leaky vacuum-pump diaphragm may sometimes permit oil to be sucked out of the crankcase.

Engine Maintenance and Repair. The most important single item in engine maintenance is *lubrication*. Other systems — cooling, ignition, fuel, exhaust — must also be kept in good operating condition in order to assure good performance of the engine, and these systems and their maintenance are discussed individually in the following pages. But for the engine itself, oil is the crucial element.

If you live in a climate where temperatures are not extreme, you can safely standardize on 10W-30 engine oil. If your owner's manual recommends another grade of oil, which is unlikely, by all means follow its teachings. And if you live in a climate that is extremely cold or extremely hot, local advice should be your guide.

The engine oil should be replaced with new oil and the oil filter should be replaced on a regular schedule. How frequently this should be done, and whether oil and filter should both be replaced with the same frequency, depends on whom you ask. Recommendations in owner's manuals range widely: from "every 4,000 miles or every three months, whichever comes first," with the filter changed every other time, to "every 7,500 miles or every six months" with the filter changed every time. Also, many owner's manuals instruct you to change oil and filter more frequently if you use your car in "severe service," but seldom if ever are the severe service conditions described precisely enough to make the recommendations useful.

In fact, recommendations vary so widely that it is reasonable to suspect that any recommendation that gets into print is based just as much on sales-department demands and clout within the organization as it is on engineering requirements. The design engineers have an incentive to urge frequent oil and filter changes, because this may make an appreciable difference in service life before an engine overhaul is needed. The marketing people, on the other hand, have an eye on the competition. If the Packillac Golden Gryphon only has to have its oil changed every 7,500 miles according to its manual, then the salesmen for the Okleberg Silver Scimitar will fight tooth and nail against a 6,000-mile recommendation in the Scimitar's owner's manual.

And if your mechanic has been to a good mechanics' school, chances are that he will tell you that his instructors told him there really isn't any reliable rule to follow.

Amidst all this confusion, a middle ground seems most sensible: we recommend that you change oil every 5,000 miles. If your car has a so-called "closed crankcase ventilation system," which it probably does if it is a 1968 or newer model, filter changes every 10,000 miles should be enough. If it is an older model, the filtering of air to the crankcase is less effective, and you would be justified in replacing the filter each time you change oil.

If you fail to change your oil and oil filter often enough, your engine will wear itself out more rapidly than it otherwise would, and you will have to overhaul the engine sooner than would otherwise be necessary. Alternatively, changing them more often than necessary simply wastes money. As this is written, a change of oil and filter costs about fifteen dollars, and an engine overhaul of modest proportions cost $500 to $800. Suppose you could know with certainty that if you changed oil and filter every 3,000 miles instead of every 5,000 it would allow you to put off an engine overhaul from 125,000 miles to 175,000 miles, would it be worth it? No. You would spend about $350 more in oil and filter changes on the more frequent schedule, in order to save $275 or so in overhaul charges.

Engine Overhaul means replacing or reconditioning all the parts inside the engine that have become seriously worn after long service. This may mean replacing piston rings, pistons, crankshaft bearings, connecting rods, and valve gear components. Sometimes the term also embraces the overhauling of the engine valves.

An engine overhaul is seldom required before the car has traveled 100,000 miles, and 150,000 is not uncommon. But even so, automobile owners tend to be intimidated by the prospect of major engine repairs, and the word "overhaul" is frightening to them.

It should not be. However much it costs to overhaul an engine, you will be ahead of the game financially if that overhaul makes it possible for you to put off the purchase of a new car for only one year; and in fact such an overhaul would enable your car to last for eight or ten more years. Consider these figures: at mid-1979, you would have paid no more than $950 for completely overhauling the engine of an eight-year-old full-sized Ford. (For a six-cylinder car, the cost would have been nearer $700.) This $950 is about equivalent to the *finance charge* you would have to pay if you turned in the Ford on a car that cost $2,850-plus-your-old-car. Looking at it from another angle, the view is much the same: the $950 cost of an engine overhaul would be about equivalent to *nine-month's depreciation* on the new car.

Engine Valves often require overhauling sooner than the other working parts of the engine, and this is sometimes done as a separate job, before it is necessary to overhaul the rest of the engine. The life-expectancy of exhaust valves is of the order of 75,000 — 100,000 miles. Your mechanic will probably be the first to detect valve trouble, because he will not be able to make the engine idle steadily when he tunes it up. (See **Tune-Up** on page 187.) And compression tests in previous tune-ups will have foreshadowed the trouble by revealing that one or more cylinders had lower compression than the others. Valves can be reconditioned rather than replaced; after reconditioning, they will last approximately half as long as new valves. If you buy new valves, the cost of the valve overhaul job will be increased by $35, or perhaps as much as $50. If you hold the long view, it will be money well spent, since it will make it unnecessary to work on the valve system again for another 75,000 — 100,000 miles. The entire valve gear is normally carefully scrutinized as part of any major valve work, and worn parts are replaced; hence the rest of the valve system is good for a full term of service.

The most likely symptom of excessive engine wear is excessive oil consumption. During the first 50,000 or 75,000 miles of the car's life you may not have to add oil at all between oil changes, but it may then begin to "use oil," meaning that the piston rings no longer form a tight seal against the cylinder wall, and oil is being sucked up into the cylinders, there to be burned along with the fuel mixture. (See page 134 for other possible causes of oil consumption.) When oil consumption reaches the level of one quart per 300 to 500 miles, as it may do at 100,000 to 125,000 or 150,000 miles, consult your mechanic about an engine overhaul.

It is often possible to restore the engine to apparently good working condition by simply replacing the piston rings. You may discover, however, after only another 25,000 miles or so that the engine must be disassembled again to replace bearings and other parts. Wrist pins, connecting-rod bearings, and crankshaft bearings also wear appreciably over the course of 100,000 miles. New piston rings will restore cylinder compression, but this will increase the mechanical load on the bearings, and the looseness that has accumulated in the bearings will cause further wear at an exaggerated rate. Long-term prudence dictates, therefore, that while you are paying for disassembling the engine, you should ask your mechanic to inspect the major parts and overhaul or replace any that show appreciable wear.

SUMMARY OF ENGINE MAINTENANCE

1. Change oil in the engine every 5,000 miles. Change oil filter at the same time if your car is a 1967 model or older.

2. Change oil filter every 10,000 miles if your car is a 1968 model or newer.

3. Recondition or replace engine valves when the compression drops and/or it becomes impossible to make the engine idle smoothly. This condition will probably be reached in the neighborhood of 75,000 — 100,000 miles.

4. Consult your mechanic about an engine overhaul when the oil consumption reaches the level of one quart per 300 to 500 miles. This is not likely to occur before about 100,000 miles. If you are lucky you may reach 150,000 miles before you need an overhaul.

THE FUEL SYSTEM

The fuel system delivers to the engine an adequate supply of fuel, in the form of a mixture of gasoline vapor and air in the proper proportions. The system also has the assignment of disposing of smoke and fumes from the crankcase by returning crankcase-ventilation air back through the combustion process. The basic fuel system consists of a *fuel tank, fuel lines,* a *fuel pump,* a *fuel filter,* an *intake manifold,* a *carburetor,* and an *air filter.* These basic elements are shown in Sketch 4. Several anti-pollution devices that have been added in recent years are described on pages 148-150; they are not shown in the sketch.

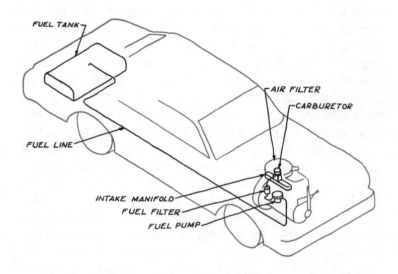

Sketch 4. A Fuel System

The **Fuel Tank** is the storage container for gasoline, usually located at the rear of the car. Inside the tank is the gasoline gauge tank unit that conveys information about the gasoline level to the gauge on the instrument panel. This is done by means of a float that rides on the surface of the gasoline; it is attached to a lever that swings up and down as the float rises or drops; and the lever operates a control knob that sends a faint electric current to the gauge.

The gasoline tank and the apparatus in it normally outlasts the rest of the car, but all of the components are repairable if need be. The tank itself is usually made of steel sheet of fairly heavy gauge, so that it can withstand the corrosive action of water and road salt on the outside and water commingled with the gasoline on the inside. Water in the gasoline is usually the result of condensation: humid air deposits dew on the inside of a gasoline tank, just as it deposits dew on grass and leaves. The **Fuel Line** is also subjected to corrosion from both within and without; and since the fuel line, a steel tube approximately a quarter of an inch in diameter, is made of thinner material than the tank, it is more likely than the tank to develop leaks during the lifetime of the car. The first symptom of such leakage is a pronounced odor of gasoline; but if you do not keep the car in a closed garage this symptom may escape you. The next symptom is a puddle of gasoline on the pavement, and beyond that will be the failure of the fuel pump to deliver gasoline to the engine because it sucks air instead of gasoline. If this happens, the engine simply will not run.

If a sizable puddle of water accumulates in the gasoline tank, either because of condensation or because you received a slug of water from the filling-station pump, water instead of gasoline may be delivered to the carburetor and cause the engine to run hesitantly and unsteadily at best, and at worst to decline to run at all. Additives to pour into the gasoline tank are available under several brand names; these liquids "dry" the gasoline by causing the water to dissolve in it.

The **Fuel Pump** sucks gasoline from the tank via the gasoline line and pushes it on, via a tube made of quarter-inch steel or gasoline-resistant rubber, to the carburetor. The fuel pump is bolted onto the front or side of the engine, and is driven directly by a mechanism inside the engine. It operates much like a human heart in that it pulsates, and on each pulsation sucks in a small amount of liquid through an inlet check valve and then pushes it out through an outlet check valve.

Fuel pumps have a high life expectancy, but it is prudent to replace the pump at 75,000 miles. When a fuel pump fails it often does so without warning and shuts you down completely wherever you may be or whatever the time of day or night. Chances are pretty good that you could get another 25,000 miles' service out of the fuel pump, but they would be progressively more uncertain miles, and the money you waste by replacing the pump prematurely is small compared with the cost of being rescued from the side of the road.

The **Fuel Filter** screens out dirt in the gasoline. It is important that gasoline reaching the carburetor be free of dirt, since the particles would interfere with the operation of the carburetor and might make it inoperative. The fuel filter is almost always located in the fuel line between the fuel pump and the carburetor, but sometimes it is located in the fuel pump and sometimes in the carburetor itself.

Dirt gets into gasoline by numerous routes, and the extent of such contamination is mostly a matter of luck. Whenever the cap is taken off of your gasoline tank at the filling station, dirt is invited in. The swirling breezes carry dust and grit particles, some of them from the surface of your own car but in any case from the surrounding roads and driveways. The nozzle on the gasoline pump captures dirt particles from the breezes and drops some of them into your tank. Similarly, the filling station's underground gasoline tanks receive dirt particles along with the gasoline from the tank truck that fills them; and the tank truck in turn receives dirt from the distribution center or refinery. Your share of all these dirt particles is picked up by the filter.

Owner's manuals conventionally recommend replacing the fuel filter every 12,000 miles, more or less.

Notwithstanding the inevitability of contamination and the many sources of it, we doubt that such frequent replacement is necessary. In our own experience of over 40 years we have not known first-hand of a single case of fuel-system failure because of a plugged filter. (We have *heard*, reliably, of one case, but the account was silent on how long the filter had been in service.) We recommend replacing the filter at 25,000-mile intervals.

The **Air Filter** is contained in the horizontal disk, 10 — 15 inches in diameter and 2 — 3 inches high, that is the biggest single thing you see when you open the hood. Its function is to screen out the particles of dirt in the air and thus protect the engine, particularly the cylinder walls and piston rings, from abrasion. In doing this, the air filter greatly increases the intervals between overhauls of the engine (page 136).

The air filter should be inspected for dirt every 10,000 miles, and replaced (or cleaned, if it is a clean-able filter) if it is dirty. In any case, it should be cleaned or replaced after 25,000 miles. A dirty air filter increases fuel consumption by causing greater suction to be applied to the liquid gasoline supply in the carburetor. (It does this by restricting the air flow through the car-buretor, so the cylinders pull a higher vacuum.) As a result of the higher suction, gasoline is dribbled into the air stream at an abnormally high rate, and fuel consumption is abnormally high.

The **Carburetor** is the component of the engine where the gasoline and the air are mixed in the proportions needed by the engine at a given time for a given purpose. The need varies greatly with tempera-ture, acceleration, and load: a cold engine requires a fuel mixture that is much richer in gasoline than does a warmed-up engine, for example; when the intake air is cold, the mixture must be richer than when the air is warm; when you step on the accelerator, the engine needs a higher concentration of gasoline, and in a hurry, than when you are cruising at a steady rate; and when the car is heavily loaded, the mixture must again be richer in gasoline than when the load is light. The carburetor must respond to all of these needs; in general it does a pretty good job.

Basically, the principle of mixing air and gasoline in the automobile engine is a simple one, and it is seen at its simplest in a gasoline lawn-mower engine. Here, the engine sucks a stream of air through a duct; liquid gasoline dribbles through a small tube into the center of the air stream at a rate appropriate to the needs of the engine. The gasoline evaporates, and the mixture of air and gasoline vapor thus formed is the fuel mixture for the lawn-mower engine.

The mixing problem in an automobile is more complex because both the amount of fuel mixture and its composition (i.e., the concentration of gasoline vapor in the air) must be varied over wide ranges to accommodate the varying needs of the engine. The essential basic operation is the same as that described above, and Sketch 5 illustrates it. The pistons and valves, acting together, suck air through the carburetor body. (The intake manifold connects the carburetor with the cylinders and their pistons and valves; this is described more extensively on page 130.) Gasoline in a reservoir (the "float chamber" in the sketch) flows through the carburetor jet and out into the air stream, where it evaporates to form the air/gasoline vapor mixture. The supply of gasoline in the float chamber is maintained at a very precise level by the float valve: if the level is too high, the float valve plugs the gasoline inlet line and the fuel pump cannot force additional gasoline into the float chamber; when the level drops the pump supplies additional gasoline.

Two seemingly mysterious but actually very simple (but nevertheless exasperating) ailments of the fuel system can occur as a result of weather. The first ailment is persistent stalling; if this occurs on a humid, somewhat chilly day it may be the result of ice-formation in the

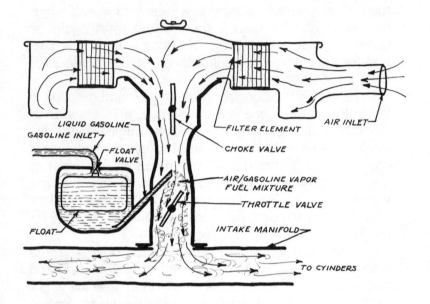

Sketch 5. The Carburetor

carburetor. The evaporation of gasoline in the air stream of the carburetor, and the very flow of air through the carburetor throat, cause some chilling of the air; and this chilling can in borderline circumstances cause the water vapor in the air to precipitate as snow or to deposit ice on the air passage through the carburetor and interfere with its operation. The second ailment results if there has been a sudden change in the weather that the gasoline suppliers have not anticipated accurately. Gasoline supplied by a filling station in the summer has a somewhat higher boiling-point than gasoline supplied in the same region in the winter; so if an unusually severe cold snap occurs, it may catch you with "summer gasoline" in your tank (or in your service station's tanks) — and again you will be plagued with inexplicable stalling of the engine until the engine gets good and warm. Both conditions will be temporary, and the best thing to do is simply endure the situation until it clears up.

Warning: Beware of Rebuilt Carburetors!

It is possible to rebuild a carburetor so that it will perform as well as a new one. Any good mechanic, and especially any carburetor specialist in a good-sized city, can rebuild a carburetor, using new parts from the manufacturer, and do a good job of it. Unfortunately, however, buying a rebuilt carburetor in our present world is all too often a mug's game. The carburetor you buy may very well turn out to be a cleaned-up fake, with a few new parts where they show, but the same old worn parts inside. Your mechanic may know a high-quality carburetor rebuilder, and if you trust the mechanic's judgment, a carburetor from this source will probably be all right. The safer thing to do, however, is to buy a new one, and save both trouble and money in the long run.

A **Choke Valve** is located in the carburetor body just upstream of the tube that conveys liquid gasoline into the air stream. The function of the choke valve is to cause more gasoline than normal to be sucked into the air stream. It is a "butterfly" valve (illustrated in Sketch 21 in connection with valves in general), similar to a damper in a chimney. When the engine is cold, it needs a gasoline/air mixture that is richer in gasoline than normal. The choke valve achieves this richer mixture by restricting the air flow through the carburetor body and thereby increasing the suction on the gasoline feed tube. Most carburetors are equipped with an **Automatic Choke**: the position of the damper is controlled by a temperature-sensitive coil spring that closes the damper, or nearly closes it, when the engine is cold and opens it when the engine is hot.

The **Throttle Valve** is a second and more important damper in the air duct of the carburetor. This valve controls the rate of flow of the fuel mixture to the engine. Since the speed of the engine depends upon the amount of fuel that is admitted to the cylinders, the throttle valve controls the speed of the engine.

The **Accelerator Pedal** controls the throttle valve. When the accelerator pedal is up, the damper is turned cross-wise in the carburetor air duct and the flow of fuel mixture is very small; when the accelerator is "floored," the damper is "wide open" and the flow of fuel mixture is at maximum.

The complexities of the automobile carburetor as compared with the lawn-mower-engine carburetor are in the form of additional features that the lawn-mower engine does not require. The most prominent and most basic of these are the *acceleration pump* and the *choke unloader.*

The **Acceleration Pump** is a device in the carburetor that is similar to a water pistol. When a trigger is pulled, it squirts an extra charge of gasoline into the air stream going through the carburetor. If you push down on the accelerator pedal very slowly the trigger is not actuated; but if you push the pedal down rapidly the pump squirts. The acceleration pump provides the higher concentration of gasoline in the fuel mixture that the engine needs for acceleration; without this enrichment the engine would probably "spit back" through the carburetor.

The owner's manual you bought with your car probably instructs you to "pump the accelerator pedal two or three times" on a cold morning before you try to start the engine. This is sound advice. When you "pump the accelerator pedal" you squirt liquid gasoline into the carburetor air duct; and so the air that goes into the cylinders is loaded with a high concentration of gasoline vapor. The engine requires a very rich fuel mixture to start when it is cold.

The **Choke Unloader** is seldom if ever identified in owner's manuals, but instructions for activating it are almost always included. If for any reason you believe you may have *flooded* the engine, then push the accelerator pedal all the way to the floor and hold it there while you crank the engine for ten seconds or so, to see whether it will start. This too is sound advice. If you pump too much gasoline into the carburetor air duct, or if the choke (automatic or manual) permits too much gasoline to be sucked into the air stream, then the fuel mixture reaching the cylinders will be too rich in gasoline to ignite. (This is the condition the word "flooding" describes.) When you push the accelerator pedal all the way to the floor and hold it there, you open both the choke valve and the throttle valve wide, and permit a maximum flow of air through the carburetor to sweep out the excess gasoline.

The automatic choke, the acceleration pump, and the choke unloader are all adjustable. The choke may need adjusting if you have to push down on the accelerator pedal more than once or twice when you start the engine, or if the engine persists in stalling after it has had 30 seconds or more to warm up. The acceleration pump may need adjustment if the engine seems to hesitate appreciably on acceleration — this is called "flat-spotting." If the choke unloader seems not to be operating at all, or if you have to hold the accelerator pedal on the floor for more than ten seconds to get the car started, the unloader linkage may need adjustment.

Other adjustments that are made on the carburetor are *idling speed* and *idling mixture*. Idling speed is normally adjusted each time the engine is tuned up (see page 187), but it may go out of adjustment for numerous reasons. This is not a difficult adjustment to make. Too-fast idling makes the car lurch forward excessively when you shift into "Drive" (with an automatic transmission), and creep forward excessively when it is *in* "Drive." Too-slow idling causes the engine to stall excessively.

Adjustment of the idling mixture is also a simple

operation and is done so as to improve the smoothness of the idling.

The carburetor should be replaced every 100,000 miles even though it seems to be working well. A new carburetor will give substantially better performance and better gas mileage than an old one, especially one that has gone 100,000 miles. And don't be worried that you are wasting money by buying a new carburetor when the old one is still serviceable; by the time you have saved 200 gallons of gas with the new one, you will have more than paid for it.

The **Intake Manifold** distributes the mixture of gasoline emerging from the carburetor to the engine cylinders. A manifold — any manifold — is a pipe-shaped fitting with several outlets. In this case, a branch or outlet is connected to each cylinder. Each cylinder sucks fuel mixture from the intake manifold when the intake valve opens. (See page 126 for a description of the basic gasoline-engine cycle.) Sketch 4 shows the location of the intake manifold on the engine.

The **Early Fuel Evaporation System (EFE)** is a recent development designed to reduce air pollution. A controlled fraction of the air that flows through the carburetor is heated by passing it over the hottest part of the engine, the exhaust manifold, so that the air flowing through the carburetor is maintained in the neighborhood of 100° Fahrenheit. The mixture of heated air and unheated air is controlled by a thermostatic valve. A fuel mixture made with air that is heated in this way can be leaner in gasoline than it can be when the air is colder: this makes possible a more complete — and cleaner — burning of the gasoline.

The **Exhaust Gas Recirculation System (EGR)** is another innovation. This dilutes the air with a small proportion of exhaust gas in order to reduce the formation of oxides of nitrogen in the combustion process, and the subsequent discharge of nitrogen oxides into the atmosphere. Since exhaust gas contains a much lower concentration of oxygen than does air, the effect of the dilution is to reduce the combustion temperature in the cylinders, and appreciably lower the concentrations of nitrogen oxides.

Both systems require routine checking at 15,000-mile intervals for plugged hoses, inoperative valves, and deteriorated parts.

The **Carbon Canister** is the device on cars of recent vintage that traps gasoline vapors that would otherwise escape from the gasoline tank and the carburetor. The canister is a container of special charcoal, located in the engine compartment. A tube connected to the gasoline reservoir of the carburetor leads to the canister, and so does a tube that leads from the air space of the gasoline tank. The canister is open to the air at its other end. Gasoline vapor that emanates from either source must pass through the bed of charcoal before escaping to the atmosphere; and the charcoal absorbs the vapor instead of letting it pass. When the engine is started, air is sucked backward through the bed of charcoal through a third tube that is connected to the intake manifold. This flow of air sweeps the gasoline out of the charcoal and puts it through the combustion process.

The canister assembly should be inspected and the filter on the open-air outlet replaced every 25,000 miles. Except for replacing broken or seriously deteriorated parts of the system, no other maintenance is required.

The **Positive Crankcase Ventilation (PCV) System** provides essential ventilation to the engine crankcase (see Engine section, page 131) without permitting the crankcase fumes to pollute the atmosphere. This is accomplished by a kind of recycling operation: the air that flows through the crankcase is not discharged to the atmosphere, but instead is sucked in the intake manifold, and from there is recycled through the combustion process in the engine. Any oil mist, or gasoline vapor that has managed to leak around the piston rings into the crankcase, are burned along with the gasoline in the fuel mixture.

If the PCV valve fails to regulate the flow of ventilation air through the crankcase properly, the engine is likely to run unsteadily at low speeds, and to stall at idling speeds. An inoperative PCV valve may also cause excessive oil consumption (see page 134).

The PCV system should be checked at 15,000-mile intervals for deteriorated hoses and faulty PCV valve, and replacements made if needed. The PCV valve should be replaced at 30,000 miles.

Crankcase Ventilation Filter. The air that enters the crankcase must be filtered to strain out dirt that would aggravate wear of the bearings and other moving parts of the engine. Cars made prior to the 1968 model year used a simple (and relatively ineffective) pad of coarse steel wool as the filter medium; it was moistened with engine oil to trap the dirt particles. This filter was in what was called a *breather cap;* and a breather cap should be swished out in kerosene, and then re-oiled, at 15,000-mile intervals. More recent engines provide much more effective filters for the air that is sucked into the crankcase. It is essential that these newer crankcase ventilation filters be cleaned or replaced frequently (15,000-mile intervals should be satisfactory unless you live in a particularly dusty neighborhood). The breather cap would continue to admit air to the crankcase; it simply wouldn't filter out the dirt if it was fully laden with dirt. The newer filters, when fully laden, won't permit the air to pass freely. The result is fluctuating air pressure in the crankcase, and this results in fluctuating air flow through the PCV valve, which in turn results in unsteady, inefficient operation of the engine, particularly at low speeds. The crankcase ventilation air filter should be replaced every 15,000 miles, unless you know from experience that it should be replaced more often.

Summary of Fuel System Maintenance

1. Inspect air filter every 10,000 miles and replace if necessary; and in any case, replace it every 25,000 miles.

2. Inspect PCV (positive crankcase ventilation) system every 15,000 miles and replace valve and/or hoses as needed. Replace PCV valve every 30,000 miles as a preventive measure.

3. Replace crankcase ventilation filter every 15,000 miles.

4. Replace fuel filter every 25,000 miles.

5. Check EFE (early fuel evaporation) system every 15,000 miles.

6. Check EGR (exhaust gas recirculation system every 25,000 miles.

7. Inspect carbon canister every 25,000 miles, and replace the filter.

THE EXHAUST SYSTEM

The exhaust system conducts the burned combustion gases away from the engine and on to the outside air, and suppresses the noise of the explosions; and in recent models the exhaust system processes the exhaust gases to make them less noxious. The simplest exhaust system consists of an *exhaust manifold,* where the exhaust gases from all the cylinders are collected into a single stream, an *exhaust pipe,* a *muffler,* and a *tail pipe.* In practice, most exhaust systems also include a *manifold heat valve,* and exhaust systems on larger engines have a second, smaller muffler (sometimes called a *resonator*) located just before the tail pipe. In recent years, an *air-injection device* has been added to reduce the concentration of unburned gasoline and carbon monoxide in exhaust gas, and still more recently a *catalytic converter* has been added to the system to carry the after-combustion process still further. Sketch 6 shows how an exhaust system is arranged.

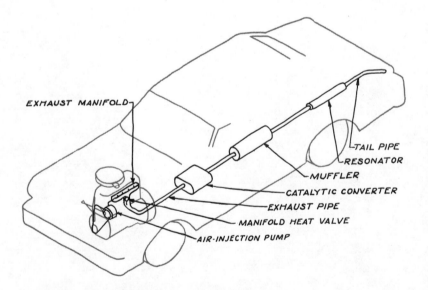

EXHAUST MANIFOLD

TAIL PIPE
RESONATOR
MUFFLER
CATALYTIC CONVERTER
EXHAUST PIPE
MANIFOLD HEAT VALVE
AIR-INJECTION PUMP

Sketch 6. Exhaust System

An important *WARNING* about leakage in the exhaust system is included among symptoms of malfunctions, on page 106. Please read it.

The **Exhaust Manifold** is a heavy steel pipe that is bolted onto the cylinder head of the engine to provide passageways for exhaust gases to flow from the exhaust valves of the individual cylinders into a common stream. V-8 engines have an exhaust manifold on each bank of cylinders. In an exhaust system that is equipped with an air-injection system, the exhaust manifold has holes opposite each cylinder outlet to accomodate air tubes (see discussion of air-injection, below). The exhaust manifold requires no maintenance, and it usually lasts as long as the rest of the car.

In an **Air Injection Reactor System** a special air pump provides a supply of compressed air, and this air is fed into the exhaust manifold at each point where exhaust gas leaves a cylinder through an exhaust valve. This air mixes with the hot exhaust gas at each point and causes further combustion of carbon monoxide, partially-burned gasoline, and unburned gasoline in the exhaust gas. The pump is driven by the engine by means of a belt, and a control valve in the system regulates the air injection to provide smooth operation. The system should be inspected every 25,000 miles for condition of belt and hoses, and to test the control valve for proper operation.

The **Manifold Heat Valve** is a thermostatically-operated damper valve that is located between the exhaust manifold and the exhaust pipe. The function of the manifold heat valve is to hasten the warming-up of the intake manifold when the engine is cold, and thus combat engine stalling. It does this by blocking the duct the exhaust gas normally flows through, and forcing it to make a detour through passages in the engine intake manifold. As the engine warms up the thermostat turns the damper to the "straight-through" position and permits the exhaust gas to travel straight on to the exhaust pipe in the normal manner.

The manifold heat valve should be checked every 5,000 miles to confirm that it still turns freely, and to lubricate it if necessary.

The **Exhaust Pipe** conducts exhaust gas from the exhaust manifold, or from the manifold heat valve unit, to the muffler. If the car has a V-8 engine and a dual exhaust system, an exhaust pipe is provided for each bank of cylinders; the remainder of the exhaust system, all the way back to the tail pipes, is also done in duplicate and there is no interconnection between the two assemblies. The more conventional arrangement is to have a Y-shaped exhaust pipe that connects onto both manifolds at the front end and, at the back end, connects onto the muffler.

The exhaust pipe must be replaced when it rusts through, but otherwise requires no maintenance. See the section below entitled Life Expectancy of Mufflers and Pipes for a discussion of factors that contribute to rusting.

If your car has a **Dual Exhaust System** you would be wise to consult your mechanic about the advisability of replacing it with a single system at some convenient time in the future. The dual system puts up slightly less resistance to exhaust-gas flow than a single system, and this is good since engine efficiency suffers from high exhaust back-pressure. In ordinary workaday service, however, we doubt that the difference in engine performance and gasoline economy is measurable, and we can testify that neither suffered when we replaced the dual exhaust system with a single exhaust system on our 1966 Ford. The saving in both money and nuisance when you have a single exhaust system is appreciable, however. In our experience, a dual exhaust system costs at least twice as much to maintain as a single system, and we suspect that in our kind of driving it costs more than twice as much. It takes longer to boil the condensed water out of two mufflers than out of one, and if most of your trips are comparatively short trips, each of the two mufflers will suffer more internal rusting than a single one would.

Some automobiles are designed with a dual exhaust system, and the purchaser is offered no choice. More often, however, the dual exhaust system was a matter of choice (at additional cost) that was intended to appeal to high-performance enthusiasts — in which case single-system parts are just as available as dual-system parts, at about the same price (or even at lower price, because of the sales volume), item for item.

If your car has a **Catalytic Converter,** the unit is located at the rear of the exhaust pipe, ahead of the muffler. The catalytic converter is a tank-like container to which exhaust pipes can be connected fore and aft. Inside is a bed of solid catalytic material that promotes combustion of any carbon monoxide, unburned gasoline, or partially-burned gasoline that may be in the exhaust gas, with any unused oxygen that may be present in the exhaust gas. The overall purpose of the catalytic converter is the same as the purpose of the air-injection reactor system, namely to reduce the amount of carbon monoxide and unburned gasoline that the automobile spews into the atmosphere; but the catalytic converter does a more effective job than the air-injection system.

"Leaded" gasoline must not be used in an engine that is equipped with a catalytic converter because combustion products containing lead compounds "poison" the combustion catalyst. Until about 1974 almost all gasoline contained tetraethyl lead to reduce spark-knock (see ignition system, page 185), and unless gasoline is labeled "unleaded," it is reasonable to assume that it contains lead. The term "poison" means to render the catalyst ineffective.

The catalyst used in catalytic converters is designed to have a life-expectancy of 50,000 miles, but not enough experience has been accumulated with these converters to know with certainty how frequently the catalyst will have to be replaced. Your mechanic will presumably be able to give you guidance in this matter.

The **Muffler** is a cylindrical tank inside of which are pipes and partitions with holes drilled in them. The muffler breaks up the pressure waves of the exhaust gases which issue from the exhaust valves of the engine cylinders in explosive bursts. The result of breaking up the pressure waves is to smooth out the pop-pop-pop of the explosions and convert it to a smooth purrrrrrrrr.

A **Resonator** is an undersized muffler that is often added to the exhaust system of a large engine to further muffle the noise that gets through the main muffler. The smaller muffler is called by a different name simply to avoid confusion.

The life expectancy of mufflers is discussed in the section below entitled Life Expectancy of Mufflers and Pipes.

The **Tail Pipe** is the rearmost pipe in the exhaust system. If the system includes more than one muffler and/or a catalytic converter, then one or more **Intermediate Pipes** are also included in the system. Like the exhaust pipe and the muffler(s), these additional pipes must be replaced when they rust through. If any of the pipes should get flattened or distorted (as by backing into a high curb, for example) it should be repaired promptly. Engine performance suffers greatly if the flow of exhaust gas is impeded.

Life Expectancy of Mufflers and Pipes. The life expectancy of the exhaust pipes, mufflers, intermediate pipes, and tail pipes varies widely, depending upon both the service the automobile is in and the local weather and road conditions. The major enemy of mufflers and related piping is rust on both the inside and the outside. Water is a primary product of the combustion of gasoline and air. This water is present in exhaust gas in the form of steam, but when the exhaust gas goes into a cold system of piping and mufflers the steam condenses to water. (This is the water you see dripping out of the tail pipe on a cold morning.) After the exhaust system heats up, this condensing of steam stops and the water goes out into the air as invisible water vapor. However, if you use your car mostly for very short trips, the rearmost parts of the exhaust system may never be free of water lying in low spots, rusting the metal inside.

Road puddles attack the exhaust system from the outside; and so a rainy climate promotes more prosperity for the muffler-and-piping industry than a dry climate; and if the local street department or highway authority uses salt extensively to combat ice and snow in winter, the muffler-and-piping people should be deeply grateful to them. Likewise, the salt in the air in seaside communities attacks and rusts the muffler and piping.

The exhaust manifold in your automobile is a heavy steel casting, and it is not likely to rust through during the lifetime of the car, although it may crack, because of stresses in the manufacturing process or some mishap in its career.

The exhaust pipe is usually made of reasonably heavy-gauge steel, and it is likely to outlast several mufflers and tail pipes — especially since the exhaust pipe provides no low spots where water can collect.

The catalytic converter case is almost certain to be made of heavy-gauge steel, since the converter is proclaimed by the automobile manufacturers to be good for 50,000 miles, and so it is not likely to rust through in less than four years. (Later cost-cutting measures by automobile manufacturers may change this prospect, of course.) But the mufflers, the tail pipe, and the intermediate pipes are conventionally made of much lighter steel than the exhaust pipe, and are subject to much more severe corrosion both inside and out.

In recent years exhaust systems have been whooped up into a life of their own by muffler shops, nation-wide franchise organizations that advertise themselves (with advertising costs that stagger the imagination) as specialists in mufflers and other parts of exhaust systems — sometimes mentioning in their advertising that they sell shock absorbers, too. Many such organizations "guarantee the muffler for as long as you own your car" — but forthrightly state that the guarantee does not extend to exhaust pipes, tail pipes, or any other pipes or clamps, or to the labor of installing any of these items.

If you plan to own your present car for another fifteen years or so, guarantees "for as long as you own your car" have considerable appeal — which at least one advertiser underlines by portraying an elderly Uncle Phud driving up in his Model A Ford to have that muffler replaced yet again at no charge — time (presumably) not permitting mention of charges for pipes and labor. Whether the "lifetime muffler guarantee" is worthwhile in your own circumstances is a matter for the same kind of careful inquiry you make about filling stations and mechanics. Obviously, a manufacturer of mufflers and exhaust pipes could make these items out of lighter-gauge metal than is conventional for the industry, and obviously it could be worthwhile to replace the muffler at no charge if the piping all had to be replaced too, more frequently than is usual, charging full labor rates. Whether the lifetime-guarantee exhaust-system specialist in your neighborhood is a better source of exhaust system parts than Reliable Old Bert — who will probably, for all his topline charges, install first-class merchandise — can probably only be decided on the basis of careful local research. Just remember, as you do the research, that muffler shops, like all businesses, are primarily concerned with their own interests, not yours. And they do spend a great deal of money on advertising, which is eventually paid for by You-Know-Who.

Summary of Exhaust System Maintenance

1. If your car has an Air Injection Reactor System, have it inspected every 25,000 miles for condition of the belt and hoses, and to test the control valve for proper operation.

2. Check the manifold heat valve every 5,000 miles to be sure it turns freely; if not, lubricate it.

3. If your car has a catalytic converter, have it inspected according to advice from your mechanic, and replaced at 50,000 miles.

4. Check muffler(s) and pipes (exhaust pipes, intermediate pipes, and tail pipes) for rust, and replace when rusted through. Life expectancy varies greatly with the kind of service the car is in, and with the climate you live in, and with the amount of salt your highway department puts on the roads in winter.

THE COOLING SYSTEM

The cooling system keeps the engine temperature down to satisfactory operating levels by conducting heat away from cylinders. Combustion of the fuel mixture in the cylinders generates temperatures of the order of 5000°F, and if the heat were not conducted away the engine would very soon stop running because of overheating, and be damaged, perhaps seriously.

An *Air-Cooling System* is found in a few cars, of which Volkswagen is probably the best-known example. A large fan drives a blast of air over the cylinders to cool them, and that's all there is to it. Air cooling imposes serious design limitations and has other shortcomings, but it is a simple system and little can go wrong with it.

In most cars the engine is cooled by circulating a liquid coolant through a network of spaces in the engine block and cylinder head, surrounding the cylinders. This network is called the *water jacket.* The coolant flowing through the water jacket absorbs heat from the engine, thereby cooling the engine; in the process, however, the coolant itself becomes hot and is no longer able to cool the engine and must be replaced by a cooler liquid. This is done by pumping the coolant that has just become heated through the *radiator,* where it is cooled by a flow of air. It is replaced in the water jacket by coolant that has just come from the radiator. Thus, this closed system consists essentially of a quantity of liquid which flows around and around, from engine to radiator and back to engine, being first heated, then cooled, then heated, then cooled. The other important parts of the system are a *water pump, hoses,* a *thermostat* to control the temperature of the coolant, a *fan* to blast air over the radiator, and a *fan belt* to drive the fan. The heater/defroster inside the car is also connected into the cooling system; whenever either of these is turned on, part of the hot coolant is diverted to the heater or defroster instead of the radiator. Sketch 7 shows the arrangement of components in a typical cooling system. On the instrument panel of the car, connected with the cooling system, is either a *temperature gauge* to report the temperature of the coolant, or an *alarm light* to tell you when the coolant is too hot.

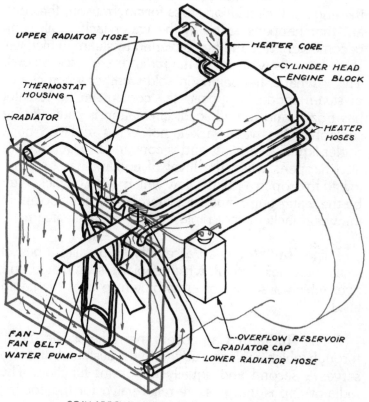

UPPER RADIATOR HOSE

HEATER CORE

CYLINDER HEAD
ENGINE BLOCK

THERMOSTAT
HOUSING

RADIATOR

HEATER
HOSES

FAN
FAN BELT
WATER PUMP

OVERFLOW RESERVOIR
RADIATOR CAP
LOWER RADIATOR HOSE

GRAY ARROWS SHOW COOLANT FLOW PATTERN

Sketch 7. Cooling System

The **Coolant** used in a liquid-cooling system is a mixture of water and ethylene glycol, or antifreeze. Ethylene glycol both lowers the freezing point and raises the boiling point of water. Water freezes at 32 degrees Fahrenheit and boils (at sea level) at 212 degrees, whereas a mixture of equal parts of water and ethylene glycol freezes at -50 degrees and boils at about 235 degrees. The life-expectancy of ethylene glycol is about two years. If it is kept in service too long, it is oxidized to a corrosive acidic material, oxalic acid, that attacks some of the metal parts of the cooling system.

It is essential that coolant circulate in order to cool the engine. If circulation stops for any reason, the coolant that happens to be in the water jacket will soon become very hot and be converted to steam, which will soon force its way out of the *radiator cap* (see below). This is what is happening in cold weather when clouds of steam suddenly appear: the coolant in the radiator has frozen and turned solid; circulation is shut off; the coolant in the water jacket, not being replaced by a cooler liquid, overheats and is converted to steam. This also happens when the level of coolant has been allowed to drop to a point below which it can be picked up by the water pump and circulated: again, the coolant in the water jacket is not replaced; it overheats; steam.

The **Radiator** is an assembly of parallel tubes of small diameter through which coolant is circulated and over which a stream of air is blown to cool the liquid inside.

The **Radiator Cap** covers the radiator filler neck, through which coolant is added to the system, but it also serves a second and equally important function. The radiator cap is the pressure-relief valve for the cooling system. The cooling system operates at a pressure of about 15 pounds per square inch, roughly the same as that of a home pressure cooker. If the pressure in the system exceeds the intended level, the radiator cap permits steam to escape from the system, just as the pressure cap on a pressure cooker operates. This prevents the pressure from increasing to the point where it would build up inside the system and blow hose connections loose, or actually rupture hoses. If the radiator cap is faulty, it permits water vapor to leak out when it shouldn't, and so the coolant evaporates away. See the section on cooling system leaks, on page 168.

Some cooling systems have a **Radiator Overflow Reservoir** connected to the radiator filler neck. The purpose of this reservoir is to prevent the exposure of coolant to heated air, which would change some of the coolant chemically, and make it corrosive. The reservoir is partially filled with coolant. As the engine warms up, the coolant in the system expands and overflows through the radiator cap and into the reservoir. Later, when the engine is shut down and it cools off, the coolant in the system contracts and part of the coolant in the overflow reservoir is sucked back into the system. Without the reservoir, an appreciable quantity of air, rather than liquid, would be sucked into the radiator each time the engine cooled down. This heated air would react with some of glycol in the coolant to produce an acidic material which would tend to corrode and damage parts of the system.

If your car does not have an overflow reservoir, your mechanic or service station can install one at low cost.

Radiator Hoses lead from the top of the water jacket to the top of the radiator, and from the bottom of the radiator to the water pump (i.e., coolant pump) which is bolted onto the front of the engine and forms the forward wall of the water jacket. Hose clamps secure the hoses to the radiator, the engine, and the water pump. The life expectancy of radiator hoses is of the order of three or even four years, but it is sensible to scrutinize them carefully every 10,000 miles, and to replace them every 25,000 miles. Radiator-hose failure is usually sudden, and it shuts you down. In addition, coolant spews out through a split in the hose and onto the hot engine, which produces a large cloud of steam. The extra cost of premature replacement of hoses is modest; shutdowns by the side of the road are much more expensive.

Radiator hoses are among the items that automobile designers and manufacturers will find hard to justify if they are ever brought to trial before God's great judgment seat. For best results you should install upper and lower radiator hoses that are made specifically for your model and model-year of automobile. A supplier of "specification" radiator hoses must stock hundreds and hundreds of hoses of slightly different length, diameter, and sinuous molded shape — and charge prices high enough to pay for this huge inventory. (For another example of this kind of consumer exploitation — in the matter of fuel pumps — see page 38.) Until all of this is set right on Judgment Day, however, that's the way it is, and sad to say, molded hoses are preferable to your only alternative, the so-called general-purpose hoses, even though it may mean that your mechanic must order hoses for your car and you must await their delivery. General-purpose hoses are straight hoses with corrugated walls that can bend and coil as needed in order to join two connections together. Most service stations stock general-purpose hoses in a considerable array of diameters and lengths, and so they are able to get you back on the road; but the life expectancy of these hoses is much shorter than that of molded hoses, precisely because they are put under severe bending stress when they are installed. They should be used only in an emergency.

Heater Hoses supply coolant to the heater/defroster unit inside the car. One hose leads from the top of the engine to the rear of the engine compartment, where it is attached to a heater connection; a second hose leads from another heater connection nearby back to the water pump at the front of the engine. Heater hose is much less expensive than radiator hose, and two different diameters supply all needs. Heater hoses should be replaced on the same schedule as radiator hoses (every 25,000 miles) since failure in heater hoses will shut you down as will failure in a radiator hose.

The **Fan** is located at the front of the engine, immediately behind the radiator. It sucks air through the radiator, to promote cooling of the liquid inside.

The fan is driven by the **Fan Belt** which in turn is driven by the engine. The fan belt has a life expectancy of three years or so, but it should be replaced after 25,000 miles as an inexpensive precautionary measure. It should be inspected for tautness every 5,000 miles, and adjusted if necessary.

Some cars have a special device incorporated in the fan assembly that disconnects the fan from its pulley when the air in the engine compartment is cold; hence the fan does not operate during the warm-up period, or in cold weather when cooling is not needed. The same device usually limits the speed of the fan: when the car travels at comparatively high speeds, air flows through the radiator without the aid of the fan, and it saves power if the fan is not operating at these times.

The **Water Pump** was given its name years ago, when water alone was used as coolant in the summer, and antifreeze was added only as necessary to get through the winter. Although the name has not been changed in ordinary use, the design has been changed, and it is no longer permissible to use water alone as a coolant because it will damage the water pump! The reason for this is that the pump requires better lubrication than water alone can provide, and if it is not adequately lubricated it will leak. Ethylene glycol in the coolant serves as a lubricant; if for some reason glycol is not available, there are other cooling-system lubricants that are also suitable. In an emergency, the car may be operated for a few hundred miles with water alone as a coolant.

The life expectancy of a water pump is of the order

of 75,000 — 100,000 miles. Leakage is the most common form of failure. (See cooling system leaks, page 168.) The other ordinary symptom of failure is a penetrating squeal from the front of the engine when the engine is running; leakage develops soon thereafter if it has not already developed. The car can be operated with a leaky water pump, provided water is added frequently enough to keep the temperature down, so you can almost always limp home. You may wish to avoid the problem altogether by having the water pump replaced after 75,000 miles.

The **Thermostat** is located at the top forward end of the engine, just ahead of the point where the top radiator hose is attached to the engine. The thermostat is a valve that controls the flow of coolant from the water jacket to the radiator in order to help the engine warm up. When a cold engine first starts up, the coolant is prevented by the thermostat valve from circulating in its usual brisk manner. When the engine and the coolant have warmed up to an appropriate temperature, the thermostat valve opens and permits the coolant to circulate. Sketch 21 on page 239 portrays a cooling-system thermostat valve in open and closed positions.

A thermostat can fail either by failing to open or failing to close. The first kind of failure is less likely, but more troublesome, because it makes itself known by causing the engine to overheat: that is, the coolant is prevented from circulating by the closed thermostat valve even after the engine has warmed up. The second kind of failure — that of a failure of the valve to close when the engine is cold — may escape your notice if you have only an alarm light rather than a temperature gauge on your instrument panel. A temperature gauge will give you persistently low readings if the thermostat valve is not closing when it should.

The life expectancy of a thermostat is of the order of 75,000 — 100,000 miles. To avoid difficulty, you would be wise to have the thermostat replaced at

75,000 miles, along with the water pump.

The cooling system has a **Sending Unit** located in the water jacket that actuates either a **Water Temperature Gauge** or an **Alarm Light** on the instrument panel. Generally speaking, a temperature gauge is designed to read somewhere near mid-scale when the engine is at normal operating temperature, but this is not invariably so. The temperature will run noticeably higher at high speeds than at low speeds, higher in hot weather than in cold, higher when climbing a long grade, and higher when the air-conditioning system is on than when it is not. (The air-conditioner puts an additional load on the engine, just as hill-climbing does; in either case, the greater load causes the engine to run hotter.) The engine temperature will also tend to run high in very slow traffic in very hot weather. This is because some of the air going through the radiator is normally sucked in by the foward motion of the car; when the car is traveling very slowly, the fan must do all the work, and if the weather is very hot, this may not be sufficient. The worst condition of all in this respect is snail's-pace traffic in very hot weather.

Important Note
about the Red Temperature Light

This light is supposed to flash red when you turn the key to the "Start" position, and then go off when the engine starts. If it fails to flash on, this means the bulb is burned out. Have the bulb replaced right away. An alarm light that doesn't work is worse than useless.

An **Engine Temperature Alarm Light** glows red when the sending unit indicates that the coolant is too hot. Some cars have an additional light that glows blue or green when the engine is underheated; as soon as the engine comes up to a normal operating range this light goes off. The "cold" light is not as important as the "hot" light; but if it persists in staying on, it is telling you that the thermostat is stuck in the open position.

Cooling System Leaks. Ideally, you would put a
fresh charge of coolant into your cooling system every
other October, say, and never give it another thought.
Unfortunately, this is not an ideal world. In the real
world, cooling systems develop leaks. You should have
the level of your coolant checked once a month or so, in
the course of gasoline stops, and water added as it is
needed. If you have to add more than half a pint or so of
water a month, you probably have a leak somewhere in
the system, and you should have your mechanic find the
leak and correct it.

There are several possibilities. You may need a new
radiator cap. If the radiator cap does not seal tightly it
permits water vapor to escape at normal operating
temperatures and pressures, when no escape should occur. This will cause the level of the coolant to drop.

A radiator hose or heater hose may be leaking
where it is connected onto the radiator or the engine or
the heater unit, or the hose itself may have developed a
crack or a split. The radiator itself may be leaking, or the
heater "core" inside the car, in which case the carpet is
likely to be damp at the front of the passenger compartment on the right-hand side. The water pump seal may
have developed a leak. There are drain plugs in the
water jacket; one of these may have developed a leak. A
very slight leak may have developed between the cylinder head and the engine block, which permits combustion gases to leak into the water jacket and force coolant
out through the radiator overflow pipe.

Some cooling system leaks leave evidence you can
detect: wet spots on the pavement, or steam, or spewing
liquid. (Air-conditioning units in normal operation drip
water to the ground at the right side of the car just
forward of the front door; do not interpret a wet spot
here as a cooling-system leak if the air-conditioner has
been running.) A wet carpet in the passenger compartment may indicate a heater/defroster leak.

Other leaks do not leave evidence. A faulty radiator cap permits water vapor to escape without leaving a trace. A hose connection may leak only when the cooling system is under pressure and the liquid may drip onto a hot surface and evaporate: again no trace.

Cooling-system leaks cannot be tolerated. If the problem is something other than a badly ruptured hose, it is usually possible to limp home, but prompt repair is essential if the car is to be satisfactory in normal everyday service. All of the components are repairable or replaceable at modest cost. Furthermore, repairs to the cooling system should be of first quality. Antileak additives stocked by most filling stations are not a permanent cure. They are touted on the label as effective in repairing leaks in cooling systems, and while they may get you home — perhaps even over considerable distances in some situations — they are no substitute for the repairing or replacement of faulty parts.

Summary of Cooling System Maintenance

1. Check coolant level once a month and add water if needed.

2. Check coolant composition every 5,000 miles and add ethylene glycol if needed to restore to appropriate mixture.

3. Replace coolant every 25,000 miles.

4. Inspect fan belt for tightness every 5,000 miles, and adjust if necessary. Replace the fan belt after 25,000 miles.

5. Replace radiator and heater hoses every 25,000 miles.

6. Replace water pump and thermostat every 75,000 miles.

7. Have the temperature-alarm light investigated immediately if the light fails to go on when the ignition key is turned to "Start."

THE CHARGING SYSTEM

The charging system generates electrical energy and stores it for use as needed by the starter, the ignition system, the lights, the instruments, and all the other apparatus and equipment that is driven by or otherwise uses electrical energy. The charging system consists of an *alternator* (sometimes called a *generator),* a *voltage regulator,* a *battery,* and either an *ammeter* or a *warning light.* Sketch 8 shows the arrangement of these parts. The word "ground" in the sketch means the car frame or any metal part directly attached to the frame, as for example the engine, the body, or the bumpers. See page 124 for a further explanation of "ground."

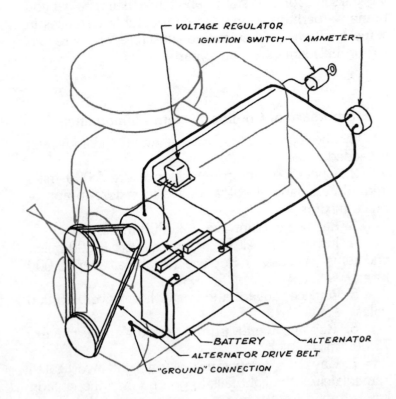

Sketch 8. Charging System

The **Alternator,** or **Generator,** located to one side at the front of the engine, is driven by the engine by means of a belt, usually the fan belt; the belt forces the alternator to rotate, and thus supplies mechanical energy; the alternator transforms this mechanical energy to electrical energy. The heavier the demand on the generating system for electrical current, the greater the resistance of the alternator to the belt drive, and the greater the mechanical load on the engine. It is for this reason that your gasoline mileage is lower when you use the headlights, for example, or the heater, or the air-conditioner, or any other electrical apparatus: the engine can supply more power only by using more gasoline.

The life expectancy of the alternator is ordinarily very high — of the order of 100,000 miles — but this does not appear to be true for all makes and vintages. Your mechanic will probably be able to tell you what the general reputation of your make is. Alternator failure is often foreshadowed by a squealing or tapping noise when the engine runs, or by persistent undercharging of the battery (see below) that turns out not to be the fault of the voltage regulator (see below). Actual failure is indicated by the alarm light or ammeter (see below). If your alternator lasts for 100,000 miles it is prudent either to have it overhauled or to replace it with a new one.

The **Belt** that drives the alternator must be adjusted for tautness occasionally; it should be checked at 5,000-mile intervals. A loose alternator belt often produces a harsh squeal when you accelerate the engine; so if you have this symptom, you should have the belt checked reasonably soon. Belt slippage aggravates wear and other belt damage, and shortens belt life. The life expectancy of the belt is of the order of 35,000 miles, but it is prudent to replace it after 25,000 miles to forestall failure.

The **Voltage Regulator** controls the operation of the alternator in order to keep the battery fully charged if possible, no matter how great the electrical drain on the battery. Thus, for example, after you draw energy from the battery to operate the starter, the voltage regulator "turns the alternator up" to restore energy to the battery as rapidly as the alternator is capable of supplying it; as soon as the battery is fully charged, the regulator "turns the alternator down."

Voltage regulators are adjustable, and on cars older than about 1966 models it is not unusual for the regulator to need adjustment occasionally. If the regulator is out of adjustment on the low side, it will keep the alternator turned down to such an extent that the battery will not be kept fully charged; and if it errs on the high side, it will keep the alternator turned up so high that it will boil battery electrolyte away to an excessive extent (see below). The only maintenance required is inspection and adjustment in order to correct a problem on either side. Models more recent than 1966 seldom need any attention at all.

The life expectancy of the voltage regulator is high: it is customary to replace the regulator whenever the alternator is overhauled or replaced.

An **Ammeter** (a gauge) or a **Warning Light** on the instrument panel reports on the operation of the charging system. The indicator, whether gauge or light, may be labeled "Gen," or "Alt," or "Bat," or "Charge." A *gauge* should point to the "charge" (or "plus" or "+") side of the scale when the engine runs faster than the equivalent of about 10 miles per hour, but at idling speed it may normally point to the left or "discharge" (or "minus" or "−") side of the scale. For a brief period after the starter has been operated, the gauge should indicate a substantial rate of charge, but it is normal for it then to fall back to a fairly low level after the battery has been restored to full charge.

A *warning light* is normally turned off when the engine is running, but it may glow faintly when the engine is idling without signifying trouble. If the light goes on when the engine is running at substantially greater than idling speed, however, it tells you that the alternator is not doing its job: it is supplying current at a lower rate than the current is being used.

A Warning about Warning Lights

The alarm light is supposed to turn on when you turn the ignition key to "On," but before you turn the key further, to "Start." If the light does *not* go on prior to start-up, it means the bulb has burned out or something else has failed in the alarm system. Obviously, you should have the system checked right away; an alarm system that is inoperative is worse than no alarm system at all.

Failure of the alternator to generate current does not require immediate shut-down. For as long as the battery will supply the electrical energy needed to operate the car, you may operate the car; nothing will be damaged by continuing to operate. This matter is discussed in the paragraphs devoted to the battery, below.

Neither the ammeter nor the warning light requires maintenance except that of replacing the warning light bulb or other components of the warning light in case the light fails. Ammeters last indefinitely.

The **Battery** is the storage reservoir for the electrical energy generated by the alternator. All of the electrical components of the automobile draw their energy from the battery.

The battery works by means of a chemical interaction between plates made of lead and lead oxide, and a liquid mixture of sulfuric acid and water. The liquid is called "battery acid" or "electrolyte." The battery has six "cells," that is, six separate reservoirs of electrolyte in which are located assemblies of battery plates. Most batteries are equipped with six removable caps, one for each cell; these are often joined together in groups of

three, and all three are removed at once from their re-
spective cells. In recent years "sealed" batteries have
come on the market. The cells of these batteries do not
have removable caps. In either case, each cell generates
two volts, so the overall voltage of the battery is 6 x 2, or
12 volts. All the electrical components of the automobile are designed to operate at 12 volts.

In normal operation of the automobile, the alternator and voltage regulator work together to keep the
battery fully charged, or nearly so. The alternator
charges the battery by causing current to flow through it;
the voltage regulator controls the flow.

If the alternator should stop supplying current, then
the electrical needs of the car would be supplied by the
battery until the battery ran down. A fully charged battery in good condition can supply the electrical needs of
the ignition system for many dozens of miles; but if the
headlights or air-conditioner are on, or if the starter is
used, all drawing current from the battery, the battery
will run down much sooner. Thus, once the alternator
stops supplying current, the operating range of the car
becomes definitely limited.

The inter-relationship of alternator, voltage regulator and battery is the cause of much mis-diagnosis of
ailments in this department. Many is the perfectly sound
battery that has been junked because the owner thought
it was dead, when in fact the fault lay not in the battery
but in the charging apparatus — the alternator or the
voltage regulator. Both of these should be checked before replacing the battery, unless the battery has obviously served its time (see discussion below). If your car is
used mostly for short trips, for example, with many
start-ups and only brief periods of running for re-
charging, it may be necessary to adjust the voltage regulator so it delivers higher-than-normal charging voltage
in order to keep the battery charged up under your
circumstances. Consult your mechanic about this.

Another familiar false alarm is caused by the formation of a deposit between the battery posts and the battery cable connectors. This deposit interferes with the flow of current. Battery posts and cable connectors should be cleaned routinely every 10,000 miles to combat this problem.

A third false alarm is caused by low electrolyte level in one or more cells of the battery. Current output by the battery depends upon contact between electrolyte and plate surfaces; if the electrolyte level is too low, then the contact area is smaller than it should be and the current output is correspondingly reduced. In addition, the plates will be damaged if they are allowed to dry out excessively. Electrolyte level should be checked no less frequently than once a month at a gasoline stop, and water added if it is needed to restore the level. (Sealed batteries do not require this attention, of course.) Distilled water or de-ionized water is preferable to kitchen sink water because the latter contains dissolved minerals that gradually foul the plate surfaces. No more than about 8 ounces of water a month should be required to keep the electrolyte level in all six cells up to normal. If your battery requires more than this, it probably means that the voltage regulator is out of adjustment on the high side and should be checked.

Ultimately, of course, your battery will die. If you are lucky you will be forewarned that the end is near and you will recognize the warning: the battery doesn't seem to be very peppy even after a long drive; or it seems to "run down" if the car sits for a few days; or it does not seem to be capable of delivering current in the amount the starter requires. If in checking the battery your mechanic discovers marked differences in the state of charge of two or more cells — with one cell showing a one-half charge, say, when the other cells show full charge; or one-fourth charge as compared with three-fourths charge for the others — you should then replace the battery, because total failure is not far away.

Virtually all automobile batteries are "warranted" for specific periods of service, and modern quality-control techniques enable manufacturers to match warranty and actual lifetime of the battery fairly well. Some manufacturers may deliberately warrant the battery for longer service life than it is likely to have, on the theory that you will buy another battery in order to receive the "adjustment" that is due you. (At least it would be tempting to do this; it would be equivalent to a slight price reduction, and perhaps well worthwhile to the manufacturer.) In order to collect on a battery warranty, however, you must deliver to the dealer a battery that has actually *failed* — that has actually shut you down; and more often than not, the warranty is null and void if the battery case has cracked, or a battery post has worked loose, or any deterioration is observable other than a simple failure to accept and hold a charge. Your own mechanic or filling-station dealer may stretch a point in your favor, but except for that possibility the cards are stacked pretty heavily against you. If you have ever tried to collect on a battery warranty, you do not have to be told that the warranty is a gimmick designed to facilitate the sale of batteries; it is intended to promote dealer satisfaction, not customer satisfaction. You may be wise to simply replace the battery as a preventive measure at the first genuine suspicion of trouble, without regard for any warranty period that may still apply. Choosing your own time, you may be able to buy a battery at a better price without any "adjustment" than you would have to pay after adjustment in an emergency.

In recent years the "lifetime-guarantee" battery has appeared on the market. Skeptics assume that this is merely another sales gimmick. In many cases, at least, the same limitations recited above apply: the battery will be replaced only if it fails to accept a charge or hold a charge; and if the case cracks because it is made of inferior material or for whatever reason, the promise is canceled. The "lifetime" that is guaranteed is the period the specified automobile is owned by the purchaser of the battery. The seller gambles that you will not continue to own that particular automobile for very many years after you have replaced its battery.

It is particularly important to buy a "lifetime" battery from a dealer you know and trust and with whom you have a continuing business relationship. Forever is a long time; and if you should ever have to lay claim to a new battery at no cost whatever to yourself, a dealer who is on your side rather than the company's may be essential to your cause.

Battery Charging can be done by any filling station: in a period of 30 minutes to an hour a run-down battery can be brought up to full charge — or to as much of a charge as it will take. If you live in a severe climate and your car must live outside night and day, you may wish to buy a **Battery Booster,** or **Trickle Charger,** for the dual purpose of keeping your battery at least slightly warm by passing a small charging current through it overnight, and adding to the total charge of the battery. Your mechanic will be able to advise you on this.

Charging System Maintenance Summary

1. Inspect alternator belt every 5,000 miles and adjust if needed. Replace belt after 25,000 miles.

2. Check battery electrolyte level once a month and add distilled or deionized water if needed.

3. Have alternator charging voltage checked if battery requires more than 8 ounces of water a month or if battery is persistently undercharged.

4. Have warning-light system checked if light fails to turn on when the ignition is turned on and the engine is not running.

5. Replace or overhaul alternator after 100,000 miles.

THE IGNITION SYSTEM

The ignition system supplies a spark at precisely the right instant in each cylinder to ignite the gasoline/air mixture in that cylinder. The battery supplies the electrical energy the ignition system needs to generate this crucial spark; the ignition system transforms the electrical energy to the proper voltage and delivers it to the right place at the right time. What happens next is described in the engine section, page 126; and the charging system section describes the supplying of electrical energy to the battery (page 170).

The basic parts of the ignition system are the *ignition switch,* the *distributor points* and a *condenser* to protect them, a *spark coil,* a *distributor* (consisting primarily of a *rotor* and a *distributor cap),* a *spark plug* for each cylinder, and a *spark-plug lead* from the distributor cap to each spark plug. Sketch 9 portrays the arrangement.

The **Ignition Switch** performs one simple function in the ignition system, and that is to cause current to flow through the spark coil and the distributor points. It performs several other functions as well in the charging system (page 170) and the starting system (page 119).

The **Spark Coil** and the **Distributor Points** act together. Their function is to amplify the voltage supplied them by the battery approximately fifteen-hundred-fold, from 12 volts up to about 20,000 volts. The amplifier section of a radio or phonograph performs a similar function — though by an entirely different method. The voltages received by a radio or phonograph amplifier from an antenna or phonograph pickup head are minute; they must be amplified many thousand-fold in order to cause a speaker to emit sound. Similarly, a 12-volt current could not jump the gap of a spark plug, but a 20,000-volt current can. The ignition system achieves its voltage amplification in this way: when the

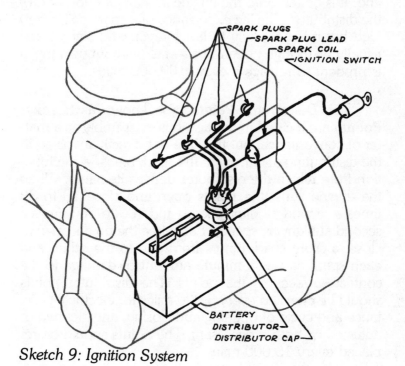

SPARK PLUGS
SPARK PLUG LEAD
SPARK COIL
IGNITION SWITCH

BATTERY
DISTRIBUTOR
DISTRIBUTOR CAP

Sketch 9: Ignition System

distributor points are closed (i.e., pressed together), 12-volt current flows from the battery through the ignition switch, the points, and one portion (called the "primary winding") of the spark coil; but when the points are pulled apart this current is interrupted and the interruption causes a second part of the spark coil (called the "secondary winding") to generate a very high voltage. In operation, the distributor points open and close extremely rapidly, and this rapidity enhances the effect of the interruption in amplifying the voltage. The very high voltage is then distributed to the spark plugs in a manner that will be described below.

The **Spark Coil** (sometimes called the **Ignition Coil**) is a metal cylinder about two inches in diameter and 6-8 inches long, with three wires coming out of one end. It is bolted onto the engine in the neighborhood of the distributor. The life expectancy of a spark coil is very high but it is not likely to last forever; and since a coil usually — though not always — fails without warning, it is prudent to replace it every 100,000 miles.

The **Distributor Points** (also known as **Breaker Points**) are located in the distributor assembly as a matter of convenience, but they are not directly involved in the distributing of current to the spark plugs — the function from which the distributor derives its name. When the engine runs, the points open and close 10 to 30 times a second at idling speed, and 100 to 200 times a second at highway speeds. Each time the points open or close, a slight spark jumps from one to the other, and each spark causes a minute amount of damage to the contact surfaces of the points. The distributor points should be checked every 5,000 miles for electrical resistance and cycle of opening and closing, and cleaned or adjusted or both if necessary. The points should be replaced every 15,000 miles.

The **Condenser** is a metal cylinder an inch long and about half an inch in diameter with a wire coming out of one end. It is connected to one of the distributor points. Its function is to reduce the sparking of the distributor points as they open and close, and thus lengthen their effective life. Conventional practice is to replace the condenser whenever points are replaced.

In some, but not all, **Electronic Ignition Systems** the distributor points are supplanted by "non-contact" points that do not touch, but approach each other closely enough to set off effects in an associated electronic amplifier and thus cause the spark coil to generate its high voltage (or even a higher-than-ordinary voltage) in the usual manner. In such a system there are no

distributor points. The performance of the electronic ignition system should be checked every 25,000 miles.

The **Distributor** distributes the high-voltage current
to each spark plug in turn at the instant a spark is needed
to ignite the fuel mixture. This is achieved by having a
rotor carry the current from a central contact inside the
distributor cap to each of several contact points located
in a circular path.

The **Distributor Cap** is the crown-shaped plastic
top that covers the distributor. A heavily insulated wire
leads from the spark coil to the center of the cap; this
carries the high-voltage current that the spark coil generates in response to the action of the breaker points.
Around the outside of the top of the cap are sockets, and
into each socket is plugged a heavily insulated wire that
leads to a spark plug.

Inside the distributor, a wand-shaped **Rotor** rotates, and provides a path for the current from the
center socket to each of the peripheral sockets. Thus
does the distributor distribute the high-voltage current.
The timing of this distribution, so that it occurs at precisely the right place at the right time, is discussed under
timing, on page 184.

Excessive water on either the outside or the inside
of the distributor cap "kills the ignition" by providing a
path for the current to leak away instead of going
through the spark plugs. This problem sometimes arises
in very rainy or humid weather when the temperature
conditions are such as to cause extensive condensation
of moisture on cold surfaces. Usually the difficulty, if this
is it, can be cured by drying the cap with a cloth. It is not
always necessary to remove the cap and dry the inside,
but occasionally it is.

Both the distributor cap and the rotor are exposed
to extensive electrical sparking in their normal service,

and in time they develop cracks and fissures through which current can leak. The cap in particular also gradually becomes more susceptible to moisture as a result of this spark damage. It is standard practice to replace the rotor each time the distributor points are replaced, but there is no generally accepted practice with regard to the distributor cap. Replacement after 25,000 miles is sensible. It may have to be replaced sooner if the car develops great reluctance to start or if it stalls persistently in wet weather. Another familiar distributor-cap problem may be found in an unsteady running of the engine on acceleration or when it is idling, but as in the case of stalling and non-starting, the unsteadiness can be caused by other things as well.

Spark-Plug Leads, sometimes called **Spark-Plug Cables,** are lengths of heavily insulated wire that conduct the high-voltage current from sockets in the distributor cap to each spark plug. The wire inside the insulation may be made of metal, but more often it is made of carbon since carbon-core cables cause less trouble with radio static than do metallic cables. Carbon-core cables are comparatively fragile, and a rough jerk on a cable can rupture the core and render the cable inoperative. The result is unsteady running of the engine because one of the cylinders, deprived of its spark, does not fire. The other thing that goes wrong with spark-plug leads is cracking or other deterioration of the insulation after long exposure to heat in the engine compartment. Again, the result will be engine unsteadiness. Your mechanic will inspect spark-plug leads each time he inspects or replaces spark plugs. They do not have infinite life expectancy, however, and traditional wisdom has been to replace them every 50,000 miles or so as a preventive measure. This practice may have to be changed in the future, however. Some 1975-model engines and considerably more 1976-model engines require spark-plug leads that cost much more than the industry has been accustomed to. You would be prudent to consult with your mechanic before replacing spark-plug leads if your car is newer than a 1974 model, so you will know what you are getting into before you get into it.

Spark Plugs provide the spark that ignites the fuel mixture in the cylinder — the final purpose of the ignition system. A spark plug is screwed into a threaded hole in the head of each cylinder. Sketch 9 and Sketch 2, page 127, show the location and general shape of the spark plugs. The most characteristic part of a spark plug is the white porcelain insulator that forms its main body. Inside the insulator is a metal rod that leads from the end of the insulator, where the spark-plug lead is connected, down into the combustion chamber of the cylinder. A second, shorter, rod is attached to the base of the plug, inside the combustion chamber. The tips of the two rods are located about 1/32 inch apart; the space between them is the "spark gap" across which the high-voltage current jumps to make the spark that ignites the fuel mixture in the cylinder. In a new plug the gap is about as wide as a dime is thick, but after the plug has been in service for 10,000 miles it is about as wide as a quarter is thick. The reason for this widening is that each spark removes a minute amount of metal — and at 50 miles per hour, for example, the sparking frequency is of the order of 20 times per second.

Spark plugs should be inspected and re-gapped every 10,000 miles, and replaced when the rods that form the gap (called the "electrodes") become too thin or too short to last another 10,000 miles. Many mechanics have by now been persuaded by spark-plug ads that the plugs should always be replaced, never re-gapped. The rationale is that the labor cost of cleaning and re-gapping a plug is as great as the price (to the customer) of a new plug — which is seldom true. The

time required to *clean* a spark plug should not figure in
the decision to install or not install new plugs. If a plug is
oily or loaded with carbon, the cause lies not in the plug
but in some other condition in the engine; and once that
condition is corrected, the plug will burn clean — and if
the condition is not corrected, a new plug will very soon
become fouled, just as its predecessor did. Solid matter
left on the plug will not interfere with its performance —
and again, it will appear in like thickness on a new plug
very soon. All that is needed to re-gap a plug is to tap the
outer electrode to bring it to the proper distance from
the central electrode. Even at obscenely high labor rates
the charge for this tapping should be much lower than
the charge for a new plug.

The genuine life expectancy of spark plugs varies
widely: it may be as low as 10,000 miles or as high as
25,000. One factor that affects this variation in spark
plug life is whether the kind of spark plug used in the car
is appropriate to the service the car is in. Spark plugs are
available in several different "heat ranges;" an intermediate heat range is suitable for most cars and most
usages. But a car that is used exclusively for short-trip,
stop-and-go service, or more or less exclusively in long-
trip service, may need a different kind, and if you are
doubtful about this, you should consult your mechanic.
In short-trip service, spark plugs often become fouled
with oil and carbon; "hot" plugs are preferable for this
kind of driving, since they do a better job of burning off
the deposit. On long trips, the combustion chamber
reaches and maintains very much higher temperatures
than it does in short-trip service, and standard spark
plugs may run hotter than necessary to do their job, with
the result that the electrodes are consumed more rapidly
than necessary. In that case, "cold" plugs would be
preferable.

Timing refers to the adjustment of the distributor
that controls the exact time at which the spark occurs in

the combustion chamber. The precise instant at which the spark should occur under standardized conditions of operation of the engine is carefully defined and published for each make and model of engine. Normally, the specifications call for the spark to jump when the piston is a few thousandths of an inch (carefully specified in terms of degrees of rotation of the crankshaft) before it reaches the top of its travel. Checking and adjusting the timing is a comparatively simple operation. It should be done routinely every 15,000 miles.

Spark Knock, sometimes called **Ping,** a sound reminiscent of castenets, occurs on an up-grade or on acceleration. Ping is more pronounced the more the timing is advanced — that is, the earlier the spark occurs as the piston approaches the top of its travel. Ping can be eliminated entirely by retarding the spark sufficiently (i.e., making it occur later); but excessive retardation of the spark causes the engine to be sluggish, to run inefficiently, and to overheat. Timing specifications therefore represent a compromise between the two extremes, and when the timing is precisely right and the engine is receiving fuel of the proper grade (see below), ping will be faintly audible on rapid acceleration or under other conditions of high engine load, but not audible at all on level ground, or at steady speed up modest grades, or on modest acceleration.

Spark knock, or ping, is the result of explosive expansion of the burning fuel in a cylinder at a rate substantially greater than the descending piston can accommodate. It can be likened to a hammer blow inside the cylinder, striking cylinder head, cylinder wall, piston, connecting rod, and crankshaft; and just as a hammer blow causes a metallic object to ring or clang, so does the shock wave produced by the fuel charge that is exploding too rapidly. If the ping could be avoided entirely it would be desirable, since the sound is evidence of abnormally high mechanical stress on the bearings inside the engine; but the faint ping of an engine that is properly tuned does not connote severe abuse, and the engine can take it without damage. You should be alert to ping when you drive, of course, and avoid pushing the engine with the accelerator to the point where the castenets are loud.

High-Test Gasoline causes less ping than "regular" grade of gasoline. Either because of its composition or because of anti-knock additives — the effect can be achieved either way — it burns a little less explosively than regular gasoline, and yet is able to deliver just as much power over the whole combustion stroke. Some automobile engines require high-test gasoline for best performance because they were designed to generate particularly high pressures in the cylinders on the compression stroke. (The higher the compression, the more power the fuel mixture generates on combustion. In most cases, high-compression engines will operate satisfactorily on regular gasoline if the spark is retarded slightly.) High-test gasoline does not yield any more power than regular gasoline, nor will it yield higher miles-per-gallon. It should be used only if regular gasoline causes excessive spark knock in your engine. It may be worthwhile to depart from this rule to the extent of buying an occasional tank of high-test gasoline to combat "dieseling," or "after-run" — terms used to describe the irritating habit of some engines to continue to run, in a snorting manner, after the ignition has been turned off. Dieseling is usually caused by a combination of factors. The most prominent cause in most cases is too high an idling speed, but a second cause seems to be carbon deposits in the cylinders: the carbon continues to glow at red heat, and the red-hot carbon ignites the fuel mixture, without need of the usual ignition spark. High-test gasoline burns somewhat more "cleanly" than low-test gasoline, and seems to burn away excessive carbon deposits. (Dieseling can sometimes be prevented in a car with automatic transmission by keeping it in "drive" until after the engine stops; in a manual-transmission car it is a simple matter to leave it in gear while shutting down, and let up on the clutch pedal if necessary to stop the engine.)

Tune-Up is a term that is widely used, primarily in connection with the ignition system, but unfortunately it is not so widely understood, and it is almost never defined. This situation can cause much misunderstanding and unhappiness. You may just have spent $52.77 for a tune-up, for example, and you may be delighted with the improvement in the performance of your engine, until you learn that your idiot friend Otis bought a tune-up kit for $4.69 and did his own tune-up in two or three hours of his own low-priced time, following the instructions on the package. You may conclude that Reliable Old Bert charged his time to you at the rate of about $75 an hour: if it took Otis three hours, Bert could probably have done it in 45 minutes, and besides Bert probably bought the tune-up kit for $2.50 instead of $4.69. You may feel aggrieved. But unless R. O. Bert has turned crook since the last time you did business with him, you probably have no genuine cause for complaint.

The trouble lies in the different meanings of "tune-up." Here is a list of 26 items that may be included in a tune-up procedure. They are drawn from the shop manuals for three different automobiles: one manual lists 9 of these steps; another, 15; the third, all 26.

1. Check compression
2. Inspect spark plugs
3. Inspect distributor cap and rotor
4. Clean or replace distributor points
5. Adjust breaker-point spring tension
6. Check acceleration-advance mechanism and adjust if needed
7. Check high-speed-advance mechanism and adjust if needed
8. Adjust breaker-point gap

  9. Check and adjust timing

10. Inspect spark coil exterior for cracks and leaks

11. Inspect spark-plug cables for cracks

12. Clean battery posts and terminals; clean battery case; check state of charge of all cells

13. Inspect and clean or replace PCV valve

14. Check all electrical connections in the ignition system for tightness

15. Make any measurements on, adjustments of, and repairs to alternator or voltage regulator suggested by condition of battery

16. Inspect all drive belts; adjust or replace as needed

17. Lubricate manifold heat valve; free-up if needed

18. Check for possible leak around intake manifold; tighten bolts or replace gasket if needed

19. Check fuel pump performance; inspect fuel lines and fuel filter

20. Inspect under-side of engine for oil leaks

21. Inspect air filter

22. Check operation of carburetor automatic choke and choke-unloader mechanism

23. Adjust cold- and hot-idling speed

24. Clean and re-oil crankcase ventilation filter

25. Check cooling system hoses and clamps and inspect radiator for leaks

26. In a road test, check operation of brakes, parking brakes, automatic transmission, clutch (on manual-transmission cars), steering gear, windshield washer and wiper, lights, horns, instruments, radio, heater, defroster, air-conditioner, cigarette lighters, and other accessories.

Your friend Otis probably did nothing more than three steps (3, 4, and 9). He should at minimum have done step 2 also, but if the instructions on the tune-up kit package were his only guide he did not do 2, and chances are that within a few thousand miles more his engine will begin running unsteadily, which he may neglect to report to you. Some other friend may have had a tune-up job done at his friendly service station for $32.20, for which the mechanic performed the Otis operations plus (almost certainly) step 2, probably steps 13 and 19, and perhaps steps 5, 11, 12, 16, and 17. Still another service station will have a different array of operations in its routine tune-up. In any case, the final cost of a tune-up depends not only on the number of items checked, but also on what has had to be adjusted and replaced.

This wide range of meanings of "tune-up" has no sinister significance. Mechanics grew up in different schools, most of them on-the-job schools, and their terminology reflects their backgrounds. Mechanic A may have been firmly taught to *always* check intake-manifold mounting bolts, no matter what, not because intake-manifold mounting bolts are often loose, but because his instructor once replaced an embarrassingly large number of expensive components on an engine before he finally discovered what had been causing the trouble all along: the intake manifold was not firmly bolted to a cylinder head, and this let air leak in, and this threw off the combustion mixture . . . . so *that* mechanic has faithfully checked manifold bolts *ever* since, and has taught all his apprentices to do so. Mechanic B may be a distributor-cap replacer for a similar reason; and Mechanic C may omit from his routine the checking of the new-fangled PCV systems because they didn't exist during most of his working life, and anyway when you check 'em they always seem to work O.K.

So "tune-up" is not a satisfactory term unless both speaker and listener know what it embraces. Naturally, you should find out what your own mechanic includes in his routine tune-up, if he uses the term at all; and obviously, you should check his list against the Maintenance Schedule (page 82) to see what will automatically be taken care of without your specifying it, and more important, what will not be taken care of.

Summary of Ignition System Maintenance

1. Check distributor points every 5,000 miles for resistance and dwell angle (page 79).

2. Inspect and re-gap spark plugs every 10,000 miles.

3. Replace spark plugs when electrodes become too thin or too short to last another 10,000 miles.

4. Check and adjust the timing every 15,000 miles.

5. Replace distributor points, condenser, and rotor every 15,000 miles.

6. If you have an *electronic* ignition system, check the performance every 25,000 miles.

7. Replace the distributor cap every 25,000 miles.

8. Replace the spark-plug leads every 50,000 miles (but see page 182 about recent-model cars).

9. Replace the spark coil every 100,000 miles.

THE DRIVE TRAIN

The drive train transmits to the wheels the force generated by the engine, and thus causes the car to move. The engine is described beginning on page 126. The drive train consists of a *clutch,* a *transmission,* a *drive shaft* and *universal joints,* a *differential, axles,* and *driving wheels.* (In a car with automatic transmission the clutch is not a separate component; it is incorporated into the transmission.)

This discussion focuses on rear-wheel drive cars, with the engine mounted in the front; Sketch 10 shows the arrangement of components in such a car. A few automobiles have the engine mounted in the rear, and a few others have front-wheel drive. All have the same or similar components shown in the sketch, but some are differently arranged.

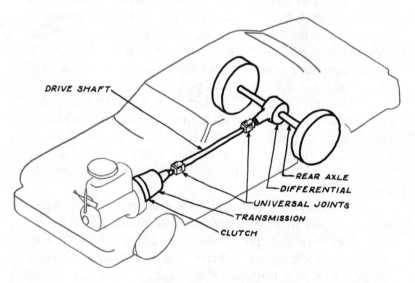

DRIVE SHAFT

REAR AXLE
DIFFERENTIAL
UNIVERSAL JOINTS
TRANSMISSION
CLUTCH

Sketch 10: Drive Train

The **Transmission.** In order to understand the function of the transmission in a gasoline engine, it may be helpful first to consider another kind of power. If we

were to substitute an electric motor of appropriate design for the gasoline engine in a car, we would not need
a transmission at all. The drive shaft would extend all the
way forward to the motor, and would be connected
directly to it. To start a car from a standstill, we would
simply feed electric current from a battery to the motor,
using the kind of control knob that is on an electric
stove; the car would then move forward. To accelerate
faster, we would turn the knob to a higher setting; and
when we got up to the speed we wanted, we would cut
back on the setting a bit and the motor would hold the
speed. There would be no need to start the motor first,
as we must do with a gasoline engine, and then shift into
"drive," or, if we have a manual rather than an automatic transmission, shift into low, then second, then third,
and perhaps into fourth gear, manipulating the clutch
pedal and the accelerator pedal between shifts. Nor
would we have to shift down to climb a hill or to accelerate faster, or let the motor idle when we stop at a traffic
light. Our single concern would be that knob: turn it
higher for more power, turn it down for less, and turn it
all the way off for a dead stop.

The major point of the electric motor in this connection is that it is capable of starting up under full load from
zero speed, and it is capable of providing any amount of
force, from none at all up to its maximum capacity, at
any speed from zero to the speed at which it will destroy
itself.

The gasoline engine differs in its capacities from the
electric motor in several important respects, and it is the
deficiencies of the gasoline engine compared with the
electric motor that make it necessary to provide a transmission in the automobile drive train.

First: a gasoline engine cannot be started when it is
under load. Therefore, we must start the engine first,
before it is connected to its load, while the car is stationary. *Then* it is ready to go to work.

Next: a gasoline engine running at low speeds can
provide only weak force. It is not capable of putting out

its maximum force until it gets up to relatively high speeds. But great force is needed to accelerate an automobile from zero speed on upward, rapidly enough to be practical. (Think of how much harder it is to get a car in motion when you are *pushing* it, than it is to keep it in motion once you've got it rolling.) Such levels of force can be achieved in a gasoline engine only by "gearing down" — a term that is explained below.

Next: a gasoline engine should not be operated at unnecessarily high speeds. Unlike an electric motor, it suffers excessive wear at high speeds. Therefore, once an automobile reaches a cruising speed, where less force is needed than was required to accelerate to that speed, it is helpful to have a device that allows the engine speed to drop back to the minimum necessary to do the job.

Finally: a gasoline engine can run in one direction only, but it is essential that the automobile be able to move backward as well as forward. An electric motor can be made to run in reverse simply by reversing the current supplied to it. In an automobile reverse motion can be achieved only by means of an appropriate arrangement of gears in the transmission.

The combination of **Clutch** and **Transmission** accommodate the characteristics and needs of the gasoline engine.

The first need of the engine is to be permitted to start up and run without moving the car, and then to take on the load of moving the car from a standstill without itself having to stop. The clutch is the basic element that makes this possible.

The principle of the **Clutch** is illustrated in Sketch 11. A flat disc, or plate, is attached to the end of a shaft. A second shaft is located end-on to the first, and the second shaft is fitted with a disc that is movable longitudinally on the shaft. If the first shaft and plate (the "driving shaft" and "driving plate," respectively, in Sketch 11) are rotating and the second plate is pushed up against the first, to make face-to-face contact, then the second plate (the "driven plate" in the sketch) and the shaft attached to it will also rotate. The second plate will not begin instantaneously to rotate at the same speed as the driving plate, of course; the two plate surfaces will slip relative to one another at first, but the second plate will gradually and smoothly come up to the speed of the driving plate. In an automobile, the driving plate identified in Sketch 11 is almost always the rear face of the engine flywheel, and the driving shaft is the crankshaft of the engine (see page 128). The driven shaft of Sketch 11 is connected with the driving wheels of the car — indirectly, as will be described later, through the transmission, drive shaft, and differential.

Thus does the clutch mechanism make it possible for the engine to run while the car stands still (clutch disengaged), and to gradually increase the speed of the car from zero to a finite speed without stalling the engine (clutch plates slipping), and finally to drive the car forward (or backward) at a speed corresponding to the speed of crankshaft and flywheel (clutch engaged).

Don't Ride the Clutch

The clutch plate is held against the face of the flywheel (the driving plate of Sketch 11) by means of a spring. When you push down on the clutch pedal, you separate the clutch plate from the flywheel surface by overcoming the force of the spring. If you apply light force on the clutch pedal, as by letting your foot rest on it — by "riding the clutch" — you partially overcome the force of the spring: the two plates are still in contact but not tightly enough to prevent slippage. Slippage is the cause — the *only cause* — of clutch wear. Slippage when you engage or disengage the clutch in order to shift gears is unavoidable: that is the primary purpose of the clutch, and this slippage will ultimately make it necessary to overhaul the clutch. But slippage caused by riding the clutch is sheer waste.

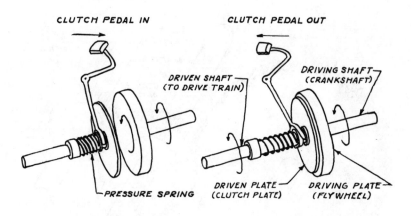

Sketch 11. Principle of the Clutch

The second need of the gasoline engine is to operate within a comparatively narrow range of speeds — a much narrower range than we want our cars to operate. This need is accommodated by selecting appropriate combinations of gears in a transmission unit.

A **Gear** is a wheel with teeth on its perimeter. If one gear is brought into peripheral contact with a second gear and if the teeth of the two mesh properly, then if one gear is rotated the other gear will rotate also. Sketch 12 shows a system of three gears that mesh together. Gear B is twice as large as Gear A and has twice as many teeth; and Gear C is two-thirds as large as Gear A and has two-thirds as many teeth. In this specific example, let us assume that Gear A drives Shaft B and Shaft C by way of the system of gears. When Shaft A, and with it Gear A, make one revolution, Gear B, and with it Shaft B, will make only one-half a revolution, since Gear B has twice as many teeth as Gear A. Similarly, when Shaft A makes one revolution Gear C, and with it Shaft C, will make one and one-half revolutions, since Gear A has half again as many teeth as Gear C.

The same relationships hold in the matter of *speed*

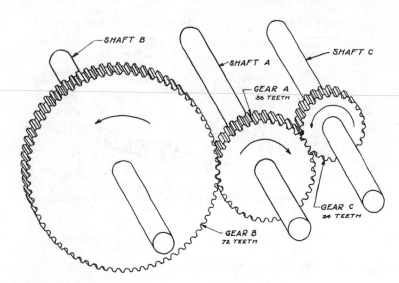

Sketch 12. Gearing up and gearing down

of rotation: if Shaft A rotated at 100 revolutions per minute (RPM), then Shaft B would rotate at 50 RPM and Shaft C at 150 RPM. Shaft A would be said to be "geared down" to Shaft B, and "geared up" to Shaft C.

Another consequence of gearing up or gearing down is to alter the turning *force* of the shaft that is doing the driving — in this case the shaft that is connected to the engine. In the sketch, Gear B has twice as many teeth as Gear A: hence A must make two revolutions to cause B to revolve once, but the turning force imparted to Shaft B is twice that of Shaft A. The opposite is true in the case of Shaft C: Gear C is two-thirds as large as Gear A; hence Shaft C rotates half-again as fast as Shaft A, but turns with only two-thirds the force of A.

The principles illustrated in Sketch 12 are employed in all automobile transmissions, automatic and manual, to enable the engine to operate within the speed range it can accommodate, and to multiply the turning force it is capable of providing.

In the **Manual Transmission,** the shifting of gears to the various combinations is done manually by the driver. When the gearshift lever is in the "neutral" position, the sequence of meshing gears is interrupted inside the gearbox — hence you may let the clutch pedal up without causing the car to move. Before you move the lever to mesh the gears together, however, it is essential that you push down on the clutch pedal to disengage the clutch, to permit the driven shaft (in Sketch 11) to stop turning. The gears may then be engaged with each other without damaging the teeth.

When the **Automatic Transmission** is set in "park" or "neutral," the engine is entirely disconnected from the drive train. At this setting, the engine may be started and operated at idling speed, ready for service, while the car is stationary. Shifted to "drive," the automatic transmission connects the engine to the drive train, in a loose way while the engine is running at idling speed or not much above, and more firmly at higher speeds. When you speed up the engine, the car moves, first in low gear, then in second, and finally in high. In an automatic transmission, the clutch is incorporated in the gear-shifting and power-transmission mechanisms; it is not operated separately by the driver of the car.

Transmission Fluid is the medium through which this connecting and disconnecting is accomplished. This is a pool of fluid which rotates with the engine flywheel; a special kind of paddle-wheel immersed in the pool rotates with it; the paddle-wheel is attached to the drive train. The transmission fluid is also the medium which causes the gears to be shifted automatically in response to changes in speed and load.

Transmission Maintenance. The level of the automatic transmission fluid should be checked, and fluid should be added if necessary, each time the engine oil is changed every 5,000 miles. If you suspect, from oil spots on the pavement or on the garage floor, that transmission fluid may be leaking, it should be checked immediately. Transmission fluid should be changed, internal filters should be cleaned or replaced, and internal adjustments should be made every 25,000 miles.

If transmission fluid leakage becomes serious, seals around the shaft at the front and the back of the transmission can be replaced.

The transmission may require overhauling after 150,000 miles or so, but on the other hand this may not be needed for as long as you drive the car, however long that may be. The symptom of a worn-out transmission is serious sluggishness (or even the actual failure of the car to move at all) that cannot be cured by making internal adjustments.

The oil level in manual transmissions should be checked every 5,000 miles and oil added if needed. The oil need not be changed; it will last indefinitely.

The **Clutch** will ultimately have to be overhauled. Its life expectancy depends on the service your car is in: if you drive mostly on short trips, with a lot of stopping and starting, or if your driving is mainly in traffic, with much shifting up and down in obedience to traffic lights, your clutch will get a lot of wear and will last perhaps 75,000 miles, or even less. If you drive on open highways where you use the clutch very little, you will get upwards of 100,000 miles, and quite conceivably double that distance. If you ride the clutch habitually, you may be lucky to get 10,000 miles between overhauls. Clutch plate — and clutch pedal — movement are adjustable and it is essential that the adjustment be checked frequently (we recommend 15,000-mile intervals). A maladjusted clutch will slip and wear at an excessive rate, just as though the driver's foot were kept on it continuously. Symptoms of a wearing-out clutch are a shudder when you engage the clutch and/or obvious clutch slippage: that is, the car doesn't speed up as fast as it should, considering the speed of the engine.

The **Output Shaft,** protruding from the rear of the

transmission, rotates in the direction and at the speed you want the wheels to turn, and transmits this rotational force via the drive shaft, the differential, and the rear axles, to the wheels.

The **Drive Shaft** is a slender but sturdy hollow cylinder that runs underneath the car from about midpoint to the rear. It connects the transmission to the differential and the rear axles. The drive shaft itself is not subject to wear, and so it has unlimited life expectancy and requires no maintenance.

The **Universal Joints** provide a flexibility in the drive train that is essential to the operation of the car. The engine is for all practical purposes bolted rigidly to the frame of the car, and the drive shaft and the rear axles are also rigid. But the rear wheels must be free to move up and down relative to the frame. (See page 208 for a description of the rear suspension.) This flexibility is achieved by inserting one universal joint between the transmission and the forward end of the drive shaft, and a second universal joint between the rear end of the drive shaft and the differential, as shown in Sketch 10. A universal joint is essentially two hinges fastened to each other at right angles. The shafts attached to the two ends of the assembly can be quite far out of alignment with each other and still turn freely without straining either the shafts or the coupling.

Universal joints are subject to incessant wear. If they can be lubricated (usually they cannot), they should be, at 5,000-mile intervals. (This operation is usually included in a chassis lubrication.) Their life expectancy is about 75,000 miles, although they will usually operate for thousands of miles after they first begin to warn of impending failure. The warning will be in the form of a vibration or a noise or both. The vibration will perhaps be noticeable only at high speeds. The noise will at first be only a clunking sound when you shift from forward to reverse, or vice-versa. Later, a yum-yum-yumming sound may develop.

The **Differential** is an assembly of gears in a bulbous housing about halfway between the rear wheels. It enables the two rear wheels to rotate at different speeds and still provide forward thrust to the car. When a car turns a corner, the outside wheel must travel farther than the inside wheel; otherwise one or both would slip. The differential gears are half-immersed in heavy oil. The level of this lubricant should be checked every 5,000 miles — whenever the engine oil is changed — and lubricant added if it is needed. Most service station people do this routinely, but don't count on it; it is better to request it specifically. Although owner's manuals usually say or imply that the life expectancy of the differential lubricant is unlimited, it should be drained and replaced every 100,000 miles.

Summary of Drive Train Maintenance

1. Check the oil level in manual transmissions every 5,000 miles, and add oil if needed.
2. Check the level of the automatic transmission fluid every 5,000 miles, and add fluid if necessary.
3. Change transmission fluid in automatic transmissions every 25,000 miles.
4. Clean or replace internal filters and make internal adjustments every 25,000 miles.
5. Check the level of the grease in the differential every 5,000 miles. Lubricate universal joints if this is possible.
6. Check clutch-pedal travel (manual-transmission cars) every 15,000 miles.
7. Replace universal joints every 75,000 miles.
8. Drain and refill differential every 100,000 miles.

THE BRAKE SYSTEM

The brake system is the combination of pedals, pistons, cylinders, cables, levers, brake shoes or pads, and drums or discs which slow down and stop the car.

Braking action is achieved by pressing a pad or "shoe" against a rotating metal surface. A bicycle hand-brake illustrates the principle: you squeeze a lever against the handlebar, and a connecting cable causes two rubber pads to squeeze the rim of one of the wheels. Similarly, in an automobile with *disc brakes,* you push down on the brake pedal and two brake pads squeeze a rotating steel disc attached to each wheel. If the car has *drum brakes,* the rotating metal surfaces are not discs but shallow steel cylindrical cups that rotate with the wheels. In this case, the friction surfaces are called brake "shoes," and when you push down on the brake pedal these shoes are pushed outward against the inner surfaces of the drums. Brake shoe action in drum brakes is illustrated in Sketch 13, and a complete brake system is illustrated in Sketch 14.

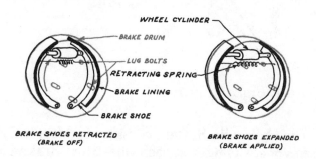

Sketch 13: Drum Brake Assembly

The **Parking Brake** on your car operates in essentially the same way as the bicycle brake. When you pull the brake lever or push on the parking-brake pedal, cables cause the shoes or pads at the rear wheels (only) to be pressed against the drums or discs. This is also called the **Emergency Brake,** which serves to remind us that it can be used if the hydraulic system (see below) fails. (It is very ineffective compared with the service brake, however.)

The **Service Brakes,** which are the brakes you use in normal operation of the car, have a different kind of linkage between the pedal and the wheels. The force you apply to the pedal is transmitted to the pads or shoes by means of a hydraulic system.

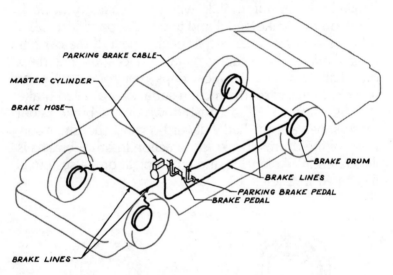

Sketch 14: Brake System

The **Hydraulic System** consists of a **Master Cylinder,** a **Wheel Cylinder** at each wheel, and **Brake Lines** and **Brake Hoses** that connect the cylinders. (Brake *lines* are not the same as brake *linings;* see below.) Cylinders and hoses are completely filled with **Brake Fluid,** a special oil. All of these components except wheel cylinders appear in Sketch 14; a wheel cylinder is shown in Sketch 13. (In disc-brake systems, the wheel cylinder is not a separate entity but instead is a component of a "caliper" assembly that also includes the brake pads and the mechanism for applying the squeezing force of the pads on the brake discs.)

When you push on the brake pedal, a piston moves into the master cylinder and puts pressure on the brake fluid in the system, which in turn transmits the pressure to the wheel cylinders and the pistons that are located in them. The increased pressure forces these pistons outward, and causes them to exert force on the brake shoes or pads, and push them against the drums or discs. (The principle of transmitting force by means of hydraulic pressure is illustrated in Sketch 20 on page 233.) When you let up on the brake pedal, springs pull the shoes or pads away from the rotating surfaces.

Beginning with the 1967 model, and even earlier in some makes, all cars have been provided with a so-called *dual hydraulic system* which means two independent hydraulic systems, one for the front wheels and the other for the rear wheels. In a dual system, a single leak or failure of the piston in the master cylinder will at worst deprive you of braking action on only two wheels, not all four. Braking action is naturally much reduced — by more than half if the front brakes fail, since front brakes normally contribute roughly 60 percent of the braking force — but obviously half a brake is better than none. When one of the systems fails, normal foot pressure on the pedal will cause it to travel further than normal, and the feel of the pedal is unusual, but the primary indication that something is wrong is of course the poor braking effect. Some cars are equipped with a brake warning light that flashes on if the hydraulic pressure in one system is appreciably different from that in the other when you depress the brake pedal.

Brake Lines and **Brake Hoses** should be inspected for leaks and physical damage at 5,000-mile intervals, when the car is up on the rack for changing oil. These lines and hoses are necessarily exposed to hazards in the form of rocks, pieces of scrap-iron thrown up from the road by the tires, and corrosion from the outside. Gross leakage will cause the entire hydraulic system to be in-operative. Physical damage sometimes causes sudden failure. Corrosion damage usually gives you warning in the form of a "spongy" brake pedal: hydraulic fluid leaks out through corroded spots, and when the brake-fluid level in the master cylinder gets too low, air is sucked into the system. Air is compressible (liquids are not), and this causes the spongy feel in the pedal.

Brake Linings are the friction-resistant coverings on brake shoes or pads. The linings provide the braking action and take most (but not all) of the wear in the brake system. Ultimately, they must be replaced with new linings; the frequency depends on the kind of ser-vice your car is in and the kind of driver you are. A hot-rodder screeching his way through city traffic wears out brake linings at a fearful rate, and he may need new linings every ten or fifteen thousand miles. At the other extreme is the sensible driver whose car is used primarily on rural highways, and little if any in city traffic. In one case we know, a car that is used mostly for long-distance, high-speed traveling and almost not at all for stop-and-go city driving, the brakes needed no attention other than periodic inspection in their first 90,000 miles.

As brake linings are worn away, the brake shoe must travel further in order to make contact with the steel drum or disc. In the case of disc brakes, the greater travel is a negligible matter; but with drum brakes, the effect is magnified and unless something were done about it, the amount of pedal travel required to apply the brakes would increase quite markedly. Drum-brake mechanisms are therefore adjustable to compensate for wear of the brake linings, and most are equipped with a self-adjusting mechanism that operates when the car moves in reverse and the brakes are applied.

Oil, grease, or brake fluid on a brake lining has the paradoxical effect of increasing the friction between the lining and the drum or disc, and making the brake "grab." Water has the opposite effect: it lubricates the lining, and reduces friction between lining and metal surface. In either case, if only one wheel is affected, its braking action will be markedly different from its opposite number and the car will swerve when you apply the brakes. The effect is more pronounced in front brakes than in rear brakes, but it is not trivial in either case, especially on slippery pavements. If all four brakes are water-soaked, braking action is very poor and the situation may be dangerous if it takes you by surprise.

Wet brake linings can be dried by applying the brakes a few times, or even by holding the brake pedal down lightly while moving the car ahead at low speed; the heat thus generated will evaporate the water and dry out the linings.

Brake linings that have been fouled with grease from a wheel bearing (usually thanks to a leaky grease seal, called a "grease retainer") or with brake fluid (thanks to a leaky wheel cylinder) can sometimes be simply cleaned off and restored to service if attended to promptly enough. Usually, however, it is necessary to replace the brake linings, and this means replacing linings not only on the affected wheel but also the corresponding one on the other side, since it is essential that braking action be identical on right and left wheels.

A **Power Brake** system is the standard hydraulic system with the addition of a "vacuum booster" interposed between the brake pedal and the master cylinder. When you push on the brake pedal in this system you activate a valve that causes vacuum to be pulled on one side of a large diaphragm; the vacuum causes magnified force to be exerted on the piston in the master cylinder.

If for some reason the source of vacuum fails, then the force you exert on the pedal will be transmitted directly to the piston in the master cylinder, but it will not be amplified by the "vacuum assist." Without this vacuum assist, power brakes are considerably less effective even than ordinary brakes; the system is designed to use the vacuum assist, and when that is not present the brake pedal gives less leverage, and hence much more force must be applied to achieve braking action.

The engine supplies the vacuum for power brakes. If the engine stops, the vacuum will deteriorate rapidly. If your power brake system seems at all erratic or uncertain when the engine is running normally, have your mechanic investigate it immediately. To be unexpectedly deprived of power in your power brakes can be dangerous.

The Brake System is the Most Important System of all: Pay Attention to These Symptoms.

1. If the brake pedal can be pushed to the floor... This means that the hydraulic system has failed completely and that your service brakes are not working. Drive carefully to a garage, using your parking (emergency!) brake.

2. If the brake warning light goes on... This means that the hydraulic system on the front wheels or on the rear wheels has failed, and your brakes are operative only on the other two wheels, not on all four. Drive cautiously to a garage.

3. If you can push the brake pedal down further than normal... This probably means that one of the hydraulic systems has failed, as described above in 2.

4. If the brake pedal feels "spongy"... This means that you have lost brake fluid from the system, and air has been sucked in to replace it. Serious further trouble may develop right away. Drive cautiously to a garage immediately.

5. If the brakes grab or the car pulls to one side when you apply the brakes... The linings may be wet from deep puddles of water on the pavement, or they may be wet from oil or grease or brake fluid which has leaked out at one or more wheels. Drive with particular

care, especially on slippery pavements, until you can get to a garage.

6. If the brakes drag; that is, if the car does not coast freely, but behaves as though the brakes are being applied lightly when they are not . . . This means that an automatic-adjustment mechanism in one or more wheel assemblies is not functioning properly and the brakes do not release completely. Have the brakes inspected as soon as you can.

Summary of Brake System Maintenance

1. Inspect brake-fluid level every 5,000 miles, at the time of each oil change. This is normally done routinely, but mention it specifically. Also, specifically request that when the car is up on the rack for changing the oil, the brake lines and hoses be inspected for leaks and physical damage.

2. Have brake linings inspected for wear after the first 20,000 miles of city driving or 30,000 miles of country or turnpike driving, and at intervals of 10,000 miles thereafter, unless you and your mechanic decide on some other schedule.

3. Overhaul the brake system when inspection indicates that the brake linings should be renewed. Unless the brake drums or discs are found by the mechanic to be in excellent condition, have them "turned" — i.e. reconditioned — so that the new linings will work against smooth surfaces. Authorize rebuilding or replacement of the wheel cylinders or caliper assemblies, and the replacement of the master cylinder, brake drums or discs, and brake hoses, unless they are found to be in excellent condition. Authorize the cleaning and greasing (called "packing") of the front-wheel bearings (and the rear-wheel bearings if your car is a front-wheel drive). See page 214.

4. Have the parking brake assembly adjusted as needed, to correct excessive travel of brake pedal or lever.

THE SUSPENSION SYSTEM

The suspension system is the collection of levers, hinges, springs, pistons, and cylinders that hold up the frame, the engine, the transmission and the body, away from the wheels, and cushion them and the passengers from the roughness of the road surface. When a wheel encounters a bump or a pot-hole, it moves — or at high speed, it bounces — up and down. Ideally, the suspension system would entirely absorb this up-and-down movement, and the car and its occupants would glide smoothly through space. In practice, of course, it falls considerably short of this ideal, but if you have any knowledge of farm wagons, coaster wagons, or other rudimentary vehicles, you know that the automobile suspension system does a pretty good job.

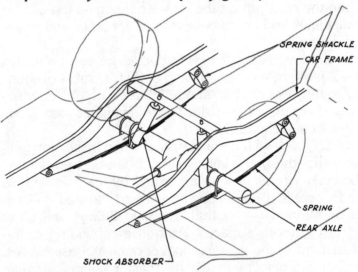

Sketch 15: Leaf-Spring Rear Suspension

The **Rear Suspension** may be simply a pair of *leaf springs* and a pair of *shock absorbers,* as illustrated in Sketch 15. The springs permit the wheels and the body to move up and down relative to each other. An alternate design uses *coil springs* instead of leaf springs. The body must in any case be prevented from swaying from side to side over the wheels. When leaf springs are used no special separate structural device need be used for this purpose, since leaf springs themselves have good lateral rigidity. Coil springs, however, have very poor lateral rigidity, and if the frame and the body rested on coil springs with no other device present, they would wobble about intolerably. To prevent this, a heavy lever called a *control arm* is included in the system.

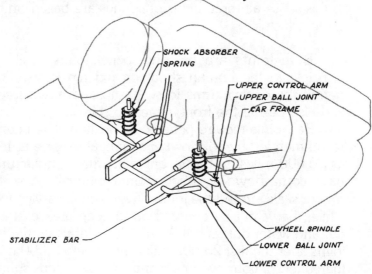

Sketch 16: Front Suspension

Sketch 16 shows the kind of **Front Suspension** that is used on practically all American automobiles. The front wheels, like the rear ones, must be permitted to move up and down; but unlike the rear wheels, they must also be permitted to swivel from side to side so that the car may be steered. It is important to the stability of the steering to hold the front wheels in a perpendicular position as they bounce up and down; for this reason, two control arms rather than only one are used at each front wheel. The control arms are hinged to the frame at their inner ends, and to the wheel spindle by means of ball joints.

Some recent automobiles employ *torsion bars* rather than coil springs in the front suspension. A heavy steel rod is mounted longitudinally on each side of the car and so connected to the front suspension that up-and-down movement of the wheels and the frame relative to each other causes the bar to twist. The torsion bar resists twisting just as the coil spring resists being compressed, and the leaf spring resists being flattened, and in this sense all three kinds of springs are based on the same principle.

Ball Joints are ball-and-socket joints similar in principle to the human shoulder and hip joints. They permit the control arms to swing up and down freely, and also permit the front wheels to swivel.

Ball joints require periodic lubrication. The interval recommended by your owner's manual may be as long as 36,000 miles, but in recent years the manufacturers have come down to much shorter intervals. After the rubber seals around the joints have been in service for a while, they can't be counted on to keep grease in and dirt and water out, and it is sensible to lubricate the ball joints after the first 25,000 miles, and every 5,000 miles thereafter. (If your owner's manual recommends shorter intervals, lubricate ball joints the first time after the recommended interval and then follow the 5,000-mile schedule thereafter.)

The **Control Arm Bushings,** where they are hinged to the frame, can be lubricated on some cars; on others they are "lubricated for life" — which is indeed true, since it means they will "live" until they wear out, and there is nothing you can do to prolong their lives. If these joints can be lubricated, they should be given the same treatment as the ball joints (see above).

Suspension-System Safety Check. The car *frame* is of course the most basic element of the suspension system, and it should be checked periodically for rust damage (particularly in regions where salt is used extensively to combat ice and snow on the roads). Worn ball joints are usually discovered by a mechanic when he attempts to align the front-suspension (see page 215), and sometimes other worn front-suspension joints are discovered at that time, too. It is possible, however, for some joints in the front suspension system to develop enough looseness to affect the handling of the car without being discovered in the course of routine maintenance. If this looseness is allowed to continue and increase it can eventually become dangerous, and the problem is that it can increase so gradually that you may not notice it. It is therefore a good idea to have all suspension-system joints and fastenings of components to the car frame and to each other checked at 50,000 miles, and every 10,000 miles thereafter. (Looseness in steering-system joints can cause unsteadiness, too. The steering system is checked on the same schedule. See page 221.) It is particularly important to have the rear-suspension joints and fastenings checked, since looseness here will not reveal itself by making the car handle badly.

A **Shock Absorber** at each wheel moderates the bounciness of the springs, and helps to keep the car steady and under control. Sketches 15 and 16 show shock absorbers in place in rear and front suspension systems, respectively, and give some idea of what a shock absorber looks like.

The body of a shock absorber is a cylinder that is closed at both ends; inside is a piston with a piston-rod sticking out at the top end of the cylinder through a leak-proof seal. The piston rod is attached to the frame of the automobile; the bottom of the cylinder is attached to the wheel assembly. The cylinder is completely full of oil; the piston has a valve in it that permits oil to flow through from one side to the other. When the piston rod is pushed down slowly — that is, when the car is riding along on a smooth surface with only gentle up-and-down movement — oil flows readily through the valve in the piston with little resistance. If the car travels over a rough spot, however, and the piston is required to move rapidly inside the cylinder, there is great resistance: the valve in the piston strongly resists the rapid flow of large volumes of oil. This resistance damps the bouncing of the springs.

The actual life expectancy of shock absorbers is of the order of 75,000 miles, but the shock-absorber industry has managed to persuade the public and even many otherwise sensible mechanics that shock absorbers should be replaced after about 20,000 miles. If a shock absorber is actually leaking oil, you might as well replace it — and since shock absorbers should always be replaced in pairs, the one on the other side, too. But beware of people who jounce the car up and down, "to see whether the shocks are working." This is *not* a good test. Genuine symptoms of worn shock absorbers — and unfortunately, most of these symptoms can also be caused by other things — are an abnormal kind of tire wear known as "cupping," excessive bouncing, body sway, lurching to one side or the other, "hitting bottom" or clacking or clunking on bumps, and wheel shimmy or "tramp." Given any of these symptoms, the shock absorbers should be removed from the car and tested, and only then should you decide about replacement.

A **Stabilizer Bar,** sometimes called a **Sway Bar,** is included in the front suspension system of most cars, and in the rear suspension systems of many. Sketch 16 shows a stabilizer bar in place. It serves as a special kind of shock absorber: its primary function is to enhance the steadiness of the front suspension, particularly when one wheel drops into a pot-hole, for example, or when the car rounds a curve and the frame and body tend to lean. The joints between the ends of the stabilizer bar and the control arms ultimately get loose, and looseness here contributes to unsteadiness in steering, and to wandering or lurching from side to side. These symptoms can be caused by looseness in the steering system and in other parts of the suspension system also, however, so when such problems arise, both the steering system and the entire suspension system should be checked.

Springs sag, very gradually, after a period of years, and let the car ride closer to the ground than it did originally. Front-spring sag, if it becomes bad enough, can interfere with the proper alignment of the front end, and even before that, sagging springs can contribute greatly to your dissatisfaction and your ultimate decision to get a new car. Rehabilitation of the springs is a much cheaper way to restore your satisfaction in your car than buying a new one. In the perspective of long-term ownership, the hundred or two-hundred dollars it costs to replace or recondition the springs is not serious; it represents only one-month's depreciation on a new car.

It is not always necessary to replace springs; they can be adjusted in various ways that will improve them. Coil springs can be returned to their proper heights at neglible expense by installing spacers between the coils. Leaf springs can be re-arched, which is less expensive than replacing them.

Wheels and **Tires** are not, strictly speaking, parts of the suspension system, but the ills and ailments of wheels and tires strongly affect the performance of the suspension system, and ailments and maladjustments of the suspension system strongly affect the performance of tires.

Wheel Balancing. Each wheel-and-tire combination used on the front of the car should balanced so that it will not "tramp" — that is, vibrate — when it turns at high speed. Wheels and tires on the rear should also be balanced if the car has coil springs in the rear; it is usually not necessary if the car has leaf springs in the rear.

Few tires and wheels are uniform in weight all the way around; they need to be tested and adjusted. This is called balancing. Weights are attached to the rim of a wheel to compensate for heaviness on the opposite side. Static balancing is done with the wheel off the car: the weights are added to make the wheel lie level on a pointed spindle. Dynamic balancing is done with the wheel and tire mounted on the car; the weights are added so the wheel does not jiggle when it is rotated at high speed. Balancing by either method is satisfactory, but dynamic balancing is preferable since it simulates high-speed service, and it is at high speeds that vibration is most troublesome.

Tire Inflation. It is important to keep the air pressure in the tires within one or two pounds per square inch of the pressure specified in the owner's manual of your car. If tire pressure is too high, traction on the road surface will not be as good as it should be. If the pressure is too low, which is more likely, tire life will suffer, and the tires will be much more likely to blow out at highway speeds. The reason for this is that "soft" tires flex more than tires should, and this generates excessive heat, sometimes even to the point of almost melting the rubber. Rubber has much lower strength at high temperatures, and so the tire simply disintegrates.

Tire pressure should be measured when the tires are cold. When the tire heats up, the pressure increases, often as much as five or six pounds per square inch. Let it. The tire is designed to take this increase in pressure — and in fact the higher pressure reduces the amount of flexing. *Never* let air out of a tire to bring its pressure down to "specifications" when the tire is hot.

Wheel Bearings must be properly lubricated, and

adjusted if they are adjustable. Most American cars are rear-wheel-drive cars, and these use *ball bearings* for the rear wheels. These are automatically lubricated by *differential* lubricant. (Sketch 18, page 229, illustrates the ball bearing; Sketch 10 shows the differential and rear-axle system of a rear-wheel-drive car.) Front-wheel bearings are usually *roller bearings;* these are similar to ball bearings except that short rollers serve the purpose of the steel balls in ball bearings. Roller bearings are adjustable to compensate for wear and thus to prevent looseness between wheel and spindle (see Sketch 16). Front-wheel bearings should be "packed" and adjusted at intervals of 25,000 miles. "Packing" means cleaning old grease out of the hub and bearing and replacing it with new grease. Many mechanics routinely pack the front-wheel bearings whenever they overhaul the front brakes. If the wheel bearings will be due for packing within a few thousand miles anyway, premature attention of this kind may be desirable, since it will reduce the work-list for the next service stop; but if the front-wheel bearings are many thousands of miles away from their next service point, by all means tell your mechanic not to pack the front-wheel bearings.

The rear-wheel bearings of front-wheel-drive cars require packing at generally similar intervals; but since most front-wheel-drive cars are European, it would be advisable to consult your owner's manual (or, failing that, your mechanic) about the proper intervals for packing rear-wheel bearings.

Grease Retainers are replaceable seals in each of the wheels that prevent grease from the wheel bearings from seeping out and fouling the brake linings. Most mechanics routinely replace grease retainers whenever they overhaul brakes, in order to protect the new linings from fouling.

Front-End Alignment is the term that covers adjustments to the front suspension to line up the front wheels correctly with respect to each other and to the road surface. This is done to make the car as easy as possible to handle, and to minimize wear on the front tires. The front end goes out of alignment partly as a result of natural wear in the joints of the steering and suspension systems, and partly from mechanical shocks when the car runs through a deep pot-hole or runs over a curb.

Alignment specifications are widely published, and your mechanic will have the specifications for your car. The three adjustments that are made in the front-end alignment are camber, caster, and toe-in.

Camber is the inward or outward lean of the front wheels. Specifications for most cars call for the front wheels to be very slightly farther apart at the top than at the bottom; this is called "positive camber."

Caster is the forward or rearward lean of the spindle that the front wheel turns on. This spindle swivels to permit the front wheels to be steered to right or left. Most cars are designed for backward lean (called "positive caster") of one degree or so.

Toe-in is the pigeon-toedness of the front wheels. When a car is in motion, the front tires tend to splay out somewhat; thus it is necessary to set them slightly pigeon-toed when they are at rest so they will be parallel in motion. The amount is small — a quarter of an inch, more or less, depending on the car.

Front-end misalignment causes abnormal wear of the front tires. Other consequences are wandering, pulling to one side, wheel shimmy, "tramp," and excessive squealing of tires on turns. Whenever you notice any of these things you should have the front-end alignment checked. It should be checked every 15,000 miles, even if you notice no symptoms.

Summary of Suspension System Maintenance

1. Balance the wheels whenever new tires are installed on the front. Balance them also when tires are installed on the rear if coil springs are used in the rear suspension.

2. Check the front-end alignment routinely every 15,000 miles, or whenever you notice symptoms of misalignment.

3. Lubricate ball joints and any other suspension joints that can be lubricated, at 25,000 miles and every 5,000 miles thereafter (but see the discussion of ball joints on page 210).

4. Replace shock absorbers every 75,000 miles if they last that long, on the theory that ride and handling characteristics may have deteriorated more than you realize, and that the shock absorbers won't last much longer anyway.

5. Install spring spacers or re-arch or replace springs if your mechanic reports spring-sag problems in front-end alignment, or sooner if you become aware that the car is riding either low in front or low in back.

6. Pack (i.e., clean and grease) and adjust the front-wheel bearings every 25,000 miles, or sooner if the front brakes must be overhauled before the end of a 25,000-mile interval. Pack the rear-wheel bearings every 25,000 miles if the car has front-wheel-drive — subject to verification by the owner's manual or your mechanic.

7. Inspect all front-suspension and rear-suspension joints and fastenings to the frame and to each other at 50,000 miles and every 10,000 miles thereafter. Also inspect frame for corrosion damage.

THE STEERING SYSTEM.

The steering system is the assembly of shafts, gears, rods, levers, and swivels that translate your turning of the steering wheel into a change in the direction of the front wheels. The steering wheel rotates a column which turns gears in a steering box; beyond that is a series of arms, levers, rods, and joints that together cause the front wheels to swivel. Sketch 17 illustrates a typical steering system.

Each of the numerous joints and gears in the steering assembly suffers a minute amount of wear each time you rotate or jiggle the steering wheel, and over a period of years appreciable looseness develops in the steering system. The change occurs so gradually that you may not even be aware of it, but in time the steering becomes much less steady and less responsive than it was originally. If you have it inspected regularly, it is not likely to become so loose as to be dangerous, but a loose steering mechanism makes a car feel old.

Steering System Maintenance requirements vary with the make and age of the car. In some cars, most or all of the joints are "lubricated for life" when they are manufactured. This means, in effect, that there is nothing you can do to prolong their lives. In other cars, some or all of the joints in the steering system are said to require lubrication only at very long intervals, a favorite interval being, for some reason, 36,000 miles. In such cases, the original factory lubrication and the seals that keep the grease in and water and dirt out are probably good for 25,000 miles at minimum. Lubrication at 5,000-mile intervals thereafter is sensible. If the owner's manual of your car recommends intervals shorter than 36,000 miles, then have it lubricated the first time at the end of the recommended interval, and then at 5,000-mile intervals thereafter.

The entire system should be checked critically for

looseness at 50,000 miles and at 10,000-mile intervals thereafter. Looseness in the gear box can be corrected by making adjustments; looseness in the joints can be corrected only by replacing the joints. Replacement of a joint is not very expensive, and in view of the difference the condition of the steering system can make in your state of mind about the car, as well as in its ultimate safety, you should make it clear to your mechanic that you want him to replace any loose joint.

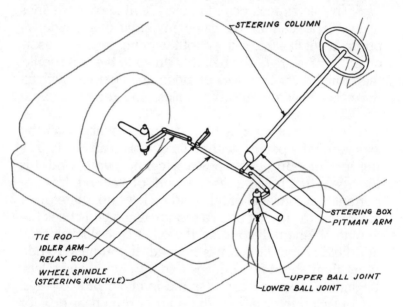

Sketch 17. Steering System

Power Steering differs from the system shown in Sketch 17 in that a **hydraulic booster** is incorporated into the system, and the steering wheel merely controls the booster. Power steering fluid (see below) under pressure, does substantially all the work of operating the levers and rods that cause the front wheels to swivel. If for some reason the booster fails to function, the steering wheel can still control the front wheels, but a considerable effort is required of the driver.

The **Power Steering Pump** and the **Power Steering Fluid** work together to provide the power for the power steering system. The pump, located at the front of the engine on the left side, is driven by a belt which in turn is driven by the engine; hence it operates only when the engine is running. When the engine stops, the pump stops, and the whole power steering system immediately dies. The car can still be steered, without the help of the power system, but the steering is much more difficult.

The life expectancy of power steering pumps varies widely, and cannot be given in terms of mileage. A pump is not likely to fail without warning for any reason other than failure of the belt that drives it; the belt should therefore be checked for condition and tightness with all the other belts every 5,000 miles, and replaced every 25,000 miles.

Warning of approaching failure is usually given by leakage of the power steering fluid. This is an oily liquid, put into motion by the power steering pump, and it is the agent that really does the work of steering. It is important that the level of this fluid be kept up; therefore it is sensible to check it once a month, when you check the engine oil, the radiator, and the other crucial levels, and add fluid at that time if it is needed. If you have to add more than about two ounces a month, you have a leak beginning, and you can respond in either of two ways: by replacing the seals on the pump or the gear box, or by replacing the pump itself. If you are away from home, on a trip where you don't have time to wait while a new pump is ordered and installed, you can have the seals replaced at almost any garage at modest cost and continue for several thousand miles more. But if you are at home, with your regular mechanic in attendance, the sensible thing to do when you discover serious leakage of power steering fluid is to replace the pump.

If the fluid gets low enough so that the pump might be damaged, the pump will make a buzzing sound that can be heard when the engine is idling. The car may be driven five miles or so with the pump making this noise without damaging the system, but it is important to get to a filling station quickly and add fluid.

Summary of Steering System Maintenance

1. Check power-steering-fluid level once a month, and add fluid as needed. Record frequency of additions, if possible, and approximate amounts added. If the additions of fluid exceed two ounces a month, consult with your mechanic about replacing the power steering pump.

2. Check the pump drive belt for condition and tightness every 5,000 miles and replace the belt every 25,000 miles.

3. Lubricate all steering system joints that can be lubricated after 25,000 miles, and then every 5,000 miles thereafter.

4. Check the entire steering system for looseness of joints, fittings, and nuts and bolts after 50,000 miles and at 10,000-mile intervals thereafter.

LIGHTS AND ELECTRICAL EQUIPMENT

The lights and electrical equipment on an automobile operate on 12-volt current supplied by the battery. Wires, switches, and equipment in this kind of system can overheat, and make sparks, and even catch fire, but there is no danger in a car of being electrocuted.

Almost all electrical circuits in an automobile depend upon what is called "ground" to serve as a return path for the electric current. (See page 124 for a description of the term "ground.") It is commonplace for lights mounted in fenders and bumpers to behave mysteriously and for the trouble to be traceable to an interruption in the path of the current, often connected with grounding. For example: a parking light is mounted in a bumper; this light can operate only if the current can come unimpeded from the battery, and then return unimpeded by way of the bumper, the car frame, the engine, and the ground cable of the battery to the battery itself. All of these steps in the circuit are attached to each other and the current flows through them. If any of the connections or attachments that make up the path of the current has corroded appreciably, then the current may not be able to get across that hurdle, and the light which is the end product of the circuit will not operate, or will burn only weakly. Rusting problems of this kind are commonplace, even in comparatively young automobiles. Once rust is identified, it is simple and inexpensive to correct.

Fuses play the same role in an automobile as they do in a house: they "blow" when there is prolonged overload on the electrical system that might start a fire or damage a component. Automobile fuses are slender glass tubes with metal ends, about an inch long or less. They are not screwed into fuse sockets, as in household systems, but are snapped into position between clips.

Most automobile circuits are protected by fuses, so if a windshield wiper or the heater blower or the radio won't operate, it may merely mean that a fuse needs to be replaced. Check the fuse first in the failure of any electrical system.

In some automobiles, virtually the entire electrical system is protected by a master fuse that is called a "fusible link." Like the master fuse in a house, the fusible link almost never "blows," but when it does, nothing electrical in the car will operate. Your mechanic can tell you if your car is equipped with one of these master fuses; often the owner's manual doesn't mention it.

Circuit Breakers are normally used instead of fuses in headlight/tail-light circuits. The reason for this is that circuit breakers interrupt the current only temporarily, and thus give you warning that something is wrong, without shutting off the lights completely and leaving you stranded. If your headlights fluctuate in intensity or go off, then back on, then off, it means the circuit breaker is responding to an overload somewhere in the circuit and is trying to tell you about it. You are not likely to do any further damage if you limp home in this condition, but you should have the problem investigated immediately because it may worsen rapidly.

Headlight Adjustment can be done by most filling stations; it is a simple job and the charge is modest. But before you have your headlights lowered, remember that heavy loads in the rear of the car make the car ride low in back and this in turn causes the headlight beams to point higher than normal. Oncoming drivers may be angrily flashing their lights at you not because your headlights have suddenly gone out of adjustment, but because you have added a heavy load to the trunk or the rear passenger compartment.

Headlight Covers, the eyelids that cover the headlights of some cars but pop up out of the way when the headlights are turned on, are caused to pop up by vacuum provided by the engine. If your car is equipped

with headlight covers, you should learn, from your owner's manual or from your mechanic, how to raise them
by hand and keep them up out of the way, in case the
vacuum mechanism should fail some dark night.

Light Switches in wide variety are used in the lighting system of an automobile. It is of course essential that
the switches for the headlight, the stop light, the low
beam/high beam, and the turn indicator be replaced
promptly if they go bad, since they are all necessary to
the safe and lawful operation of the car. All the other
switches can be replaced, too, generally speaking at
modest cost; so there is no need to get along without
passenger-compartment lights, trunk lights, glove-
compartment lights, and other lights that make your car
easier and pleasanter to drive. By all means have them
replaced promptly if they fail; their presence or absence
can make a big difference in your state of mind.

The **Turn-Signal Switch** is located underneath the
steering wheel. It is one of the few switches that is expensive to replace, since the steering wheel must be
removed to get at it, and the switch assembly itself is
more expensive than most. Failure of the turn-indicator
switch most often takes the form of failure of the "can-
celing" mechanism — that is, the turning-off of the sig-
nals after you have made the turn. The mechanism depends on a piece of tough, resilient plastic; it will last for
many years if it is not abused, and you can add im-
measurably to its life expectancy if you will refrain from
keeping your finger on the lever after you have switched
it on. The turn-signal lever should not be restrained from
returning to neutral, since this puts great strain on the
mechanism. You can reduce the likelihood of your ever
having to repair the turn-signal switch if you will develop
the habit of returning it to neutral manually.

The **Windshield Wiper** and the **Windshield
Washer** are usually combined into a single unit. The

same electric motor that causes the wiper blades to move back and forth also drives a small water pump that squirts water through tubing and jets to the windshield. The motor and wiper mechanism are ruggedly built and normally last indefinitely. The water pump usually contains rubber or plastic check valves, and these may have to be replaced once or twice during the lifetime of the car. The only other windshield washer problem that you are likely to encounter comes from the plugging-up of the jets. These can usually be cleaned out with a fine wire or a pin of small diameter, without disassembling the jet assembly; but even if more extensive cleaning is required, it is a comparatively simple job.

Windshield Washers Require Antifreeze in Winter. Radiator antifreeze is not satisfactory for this service because it leaves gummy materials behind when it evaporates. Special antifreeze compounds are made for windshield washers.

Windshield Wiper Blades become smeary as they wear out, but a smeary blade is not necessarily worn — it may merely be fouled with oil and dirt. Automobiles travel in a cloud of oil mist that is sprayed in the air by all automobiles. The wiping edge of the windshield wiper blade picks up oil from the air and from the windshield, and the oil layer traps particles of dust and grit that prevent the blade from making good contact with the glass. Filling-station attendants seldom if ever clean the blades, however conscientious they may be about cleaning the windshield itself. Kitchen scouring powder is effective on wiper blades — but you may have to do this job yourself.

The **Heater,** the **Defroster,** and the **Air-Conditioner** are usually connected together in a single unit that uses a single electric blower to deliver either heater or cooled air through a system of ducts. Most present-day systems automatically turn on the heater or the air-conditioner, as appropriate, in response to the setting of the control thermostat.

The system operates with two radiators, one for heating and one for cooling. When you set the controls to "heat," hot water from the engine flows through a small radiator, known as the heater core. Air is blown over this hot surface, warmed, and then blown out into the passenger compartment. When you set the control to "defrost," you cause a damper valve in the duct system to divert the warmed air to narrow slits underneath the windshield.

When you set the controls to "cool," chilled refrigerant flows into the cooling radiator. Air is blown over the cold surface, cooled, and then blown out into the passenger compartment.

Air-conditioning requires a considerable amount of power, and for this reason affects the fuel consumption of the car quite considerably. The blower, of course, requires some power, but by far the greater power requirement is for operating the compressor that sucks refrigerant vapor from the refrigeration core and compresses it to convert it to a liquid. Thus, if you can use the blower alone for cooling on some occasions, you can save somewhat on your gas consumption.

The heater/defroster components of the unit do not require routine maintenance, nor does the blower. The refrigeration component requires attention periodically because refrigerant can leak out of the system. It is sensible, therefore, to have the system checked every 10,000 miles for condition of hoses, refrigerant level, and leaks. This inspection can also be scheduled on a calendar basis — say every spring — but the mileage basis should work out equally well in ordinary conditions. The air-conditioning unit should also be operated at maximum cooling setting for a minimum of five minutes once every month, in winter as well as in summer, to circulate the refrigerant and the oil that is mixed with it through the system. This will lubricate the seals and maintain them in condition longer than would be the case if they were not lubricated.

The **Power Seat** is moved back and forth and up and down by a heavy-duty electric motor and appropriate gears, levers, and screw threads underneath the seat. The motor and accompanying mechanism are ruggedly built and not likely to fail during the lifetime of the car. The control switch with which the driver controls the mechanism is also ruggedly built, and if the unit fails to work, you should suspect the fuse before you ask the mechanic to repair the switch. Once you know the fuse is not the culprit, then ask him to go after the switch. It is not likely to be the motor or any other part of the seat assembly.

If the action of the power seat should become sluggish, or its range of movement reduced, the mechanism should be cleaned and oiled. The seat mechanism is located where dust and dirt are at their thickest.

Power Windows, Power Antennas, Convertible Tops and similar mechanized apparatus are usually, like the power seat, provided with motors and drive mechanisms of rugged construction and long life expectancy. As in the case of the power seat, when you have trouble with these things, the fuse should be checked first and the control switch next, before you begin to suspect the mechanism itself.

Summary of Maintenance

1. Once a month, winter and summer, operate the air-conditioning unit at maximum setting for at least five minutes, to circulate the refrigerant and the oil.

2. Every 10,000 miles, or every spring, have the air-conditioning unit checked for condition of hoses, refrigerant level, and refrigerant leaks.

3. Add antifreeze to the windshield-washer solution if you are likely to encounter freezing weather.

13. SOME DEFINITIONS

Axle: In ordinary automobile usage, the axle — or more precisely, the pair of axles — are those shafts (see page 237) that drive and rotate with the drive wheels. These are the rear wheels in a rear-wheel-drive car and the front wheels in a front-wheel-drive car. The spindle on which the front wheels rotate (in a rear-wheel-drive car) are not called axles, but instead are called *wheel spindles or steering knuckles.* (See Sketch 16, page 209.)

Bearing: Any carefully-sized hole that guides a rotating shaft or rod or wheel so that it will rotate without wobble. Sketch 18a shows a *sleeve bearing;* the purpose of this bearing is to permit the shaft and the wheel attached to it to rotate. A large number of different kinds of bearings are used in an automobile: wheel bearings, and bearings that permit and guide the rotation of the fan, the alternator, the air-conditioner compressor, among others. The windshield-wiper arm swings to and fro on a bearing. The window crank is held in proper position and made to turn true by a bearing inside the door. The speedometer needle is attached to a shaft that is held in

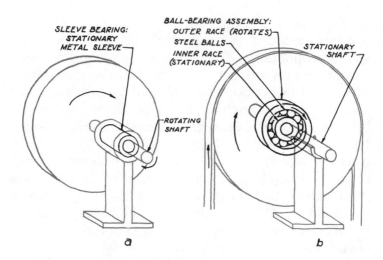

Sketch 18. Two Kinds of Bearings

position and permitted to turn by a suitable bearing.

Bearings are usually made of special low-friction wear-resistant materials, particularly certain kinds of bronze and special plastics.

The lowest friction and maximum service life are achieved in the variety of bearings known as *ball bearings* or *roller bearings.* Ball bearings are shown in Sketch 18b, where the ball bearing permits the wheel to rotate on a shaft that is held stationary. Roller bearings are generally similar: the steel balls are replaced by short cylinders. The overall effect is the same: the outer doughnut is separated from the inner doughnut by the rollers, and the two doughnuts can rotate relative to one another, with little friction, because the rollers between them roll freely.

Bushing: A particular kind of bearing (see above). A bushing is a sleeve bearing that holds and guides a shaft that rotates back and forth rather than around and around. Thus the shaft of of a windshield-wiper blade would be said to be mounted in a bushing rather than in a bearing.

Cable: In general usage, a strong wire, rope or chain. In automobile usage, a cable is always mentioned in a specific connotation. Thus: *a spark-plug lead* is sometimes called a *spark cable,* and it means a heavily insulated wire that conducts current from the distributor to a spark plug (see Sketch 9, page 179). *Battery cables* are insulated thick wires that carry heavy currents from the battery to the starter (Sketch 1, page 119) and to all electrical components of the automobile. *Jumper cables* are heavy-duty insulated wires similar to battery cables fitted with clamps at their ends; they are used in rescue operations to start an engine when the battery won't do its job. The *brake cable* is a steel connecting link between the parking-brake lever or pedal and the rear brakes (Sketch 14, page 202). The *speedometer cable* transmits the rotational speed of the automobile wheels, via the drive shaft, to the speedometer, so that the speedometer can indicate both speed and distance traveled.

Cam: Sketches 19 and 21c together show what a cam is and how it works to cause the valves in an automobile engine to open and close. As the camshaft (Sketch 19) turns, it brings the cam around so that its highest point, called the lobe, is in position to force a pushrod that is riding on it to rise higher than it was previously. Sketches 19 and 21c also show the rocker arm. As the lobe forces the pushrod to rise, the pushrod forces the rocker arm to rock, and the rocker arm in turn forces the engine valve (page 239) to open against the resistance of the valve spring.

   This description of a cam may be generalized by defining it as a disk (of whatever shape) mounted on a shaft in such a manner that a pushrod or other "cam follower" riding on its periphery is caused to rise and fall as the shaft and disk rotate (or move or swing in and out if the shaft is vertical). Thus, a cam may be a circular disk mounted off-center on a shaft. It may also be a square disk with the shaft running through its center. This is the

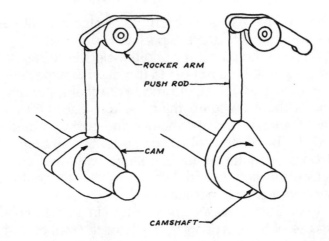

Sketch 19. Cam

kind of cam that is used in the distributor of a four-cylinder engine: with each revolution of the camshaft, an arm that presses against the periphery of the cam swings in and out four times. In an eight-cylinder engine, the disk mounted on the shaft is octagonal in shape, so the cam follower swings in and out eight times for each revolution of the camshaft.

Circuit: In an automobile, the word pertains to electrical circuits exclusively. The basic idea in its simplest version is this: if you connect a wire onto the two poles, or posts, of a live battery, current will flow through the wire from one post to the other. If the wire from the first post goes not simply to the other post but instead to a light bulb, for example, and then a second wire goes from the light bulb to the other post of the battery, the current will flow from the battery through the light bulb, causing it to light up, and then back to the battery. If an electric motor is interposed in the path from one battery post to the other, then the electric current will flow through the motor and cause it to run. These simple illustrations may be generalized this way: an electrical circuit is an electrical path from one post of a battery to the other, without regard for what useful function the electric current passing through the circuit is expected to do.

Since in the practical world the electric current that flows from one battery post to the other is expected to do something useful, an electrical path that is permitted to flow without doing anything useful is called a *short-circuit*. Thus a wire that connects one post of a battery directly to the other would divert current away from any light bulb or motor in an alternative path, and so the direct connection would "short-circuit" the bulb or motor and render it inoperative.

Most, but not all, electrical circuits in an automobile make use of the steel engine block, or the frame, or the body, or some other structural member which is capable of conducting electric current. Thus, if a wire connects one post of the battery to a light bulb, a second wire connects the light bulb with the frame of the car, and a third wire connects the frame of the car with the other post of the battery, then these elements together will constitute an electrical circuit. In any electrical circuit that depends upon frame, body, or engine for part of its electrical path, any connection to the frame, body, or engine is called a *ground* connection. (See page 124.)

Cylinder and piston: Categorically, any hole occupied by a movable plug that fits the hole reasonably snugly is a cylinder-and-piston assembly. In practice, one or both ends of the hole are capped, and fitted with pipes or tubes, so that a liquid or gas can be pushed out or sucked in by the piston, and made to perform some useful function. Sketch 20 illustrates two cylinder-and-piston assemblies.

The one at the left (20a) is a simple bicycle pump. When you pull up on the handle, the check valve at the bottom of the cylinder prevents air from being sucked into the cylinder via the hose, and so air flows around the piston (a simple leather cup) instead. When you push down on the handle, the leather cup resists leakage of air in the upward direction but the check valve does not resist the flow of air: the ball drops downward, out of the hole it has been plugging, and air is permitted to flow freely through the hose.

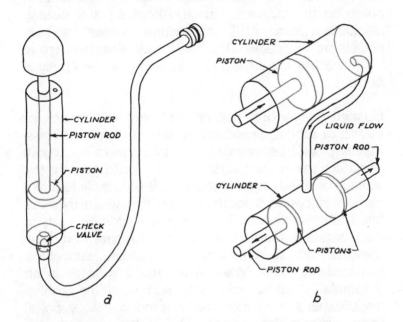

Sketch 20. Two Cylinder-and-Piston Assemblies

The assembly shown in Sketch 20b illustrates how mechanical force may be transmitted hydraulically. If the upper cylinder is filled with oil, force on the piston rod will cause the piston to move into the upper cylinder and this will force oil into the lower cylinder. This flow will result in the pistons and piston rods of the lower cylinder being forced outward. Thus, mechanical force applied to the upper piston rod will cause the lower piston rods to exert mechanical force in their turn. Contrarily, if the piston in the upper cylinder is pulled outward, oil will be sucked from the lower piston into the upper one, and in consequence the pistons in the lower cylinder will be pulled inward.

There are many different cylinder-and-piston assemblies in an automobile. The brake system (page 201) employs inter-connected cylinders similar to the combination shown in Sketch 20b. The basic operation of an internal-combustion engine (Sketch 2, page 127) depends upon a cylinder-and-piston assembly. The acceleration pump on the carburetor (page 146, the power-steering mechanism (page 219), the vacuum booster used on power brakes (page 205), the shock absorbers (page 211)—each of these has a cylinder-and-piston assembly at its heart.

Gasket: A layer of paper, or cardboard, or asbestos, or plastic, or rubber, or soft metal such as copper or brass, that is placed between two metal surfaces to absorb imperfections in their surfaces and thus to prevent the leakage of liquid or gas at the joint. It is possible to make metal surfaces so smooth and flat that when they are fitted together they will not permit liquids or gases to pass between them, even under comparatively high pressure. But such surfaces are scientific curiosities. Hundreds of joints between flat metal surfaces in an automobile must be leakproof, and it would be prohibitively expensive to machine or sand or file or polish these surfaces flat enough. The gasket comes to the rescue.

Gear: The simplest definition of a gear is "a toothed wheel," and such a simple gear is shown in Sketch 12 on page 196. Few gears in an automobile are as simple as the ones portrayed; the shapes of gear teeth are ordinarily much more sophisticated than those in the sketch, to reduce the noise of gear contact, and to spread wear of the gear teeth over wider areas of contact.

Grease retainer: A few *seals* (see page 236) are called grease retainers as a matter of usage, not of substance. The most familiar example is a grease-retainer in the hub of the front or rear wheel of an automobile. The wheel bearings must be lubricated with grease, but the grease must not be permitted to seep onto the brake linings (see page 204), and so a seal is required; in this case, the seal is called a "retainer."

Grease vs. oil: Generally speaking, grease is a thickened oil — that is, it is oil to which thickener has been added to give it greater body and to prevent its flowing away from the spot where it is needed. Both oil and grease are used for lubricating joints, gears, bearings, and other points of contact where surfaces would wear if they were not covered with a film of oil. The lubricating liquid that is put in an engine crankcase (page 131) is invariably called *oil;* the lubricant that is squirted into steering-system and suspension-system joints in a chassis lube is invariably called *grease.* In between there are a few borderline cases: the lubricant that is used in the differential, for example, (see page 200) may be called either oil or grease, depending upon local usage, and so may the lubricant that is used in manual transmissions (page 196). Automatic-transmission *fluid* serves a lubricating function, but it is not primarily a lubricant; it is never called either "oil" or "grease," but "fluid."

Hydraulic system: The basic concept of the hydraulic system is to transmit force or motion by causing a liquid to flow from one point in a system to another. The most familiar embodiment of the concept in an automobile is in the brake system (Sketch 14, page 202): the master cylinder, which is in effect a pump, forces liquid through pipes into the wheel cylinders, which then forces the pistons outward. (This principle is also illustrated in Sketch 20b.) In the power-steering system (see page 219), the pump is operated by a belt; the pump builds up pressure in a liquid reservoir, and this liquid under pressure and controlled by the steering wheel forces its way into a cylinder and causes a piston to move.

Linkage: In an automobile, the term means a rod or a lever, or a combination of rods and levers, with appropriate ends for fastening to other components. Thus, the *clutch linkage* is the array of levers and pushrods that transmits motion of the clutch pedal to the clutch plate (see Sketch 11, page 195, for a simplified illustration); and the *steering linkage* is the collection of levers and pushrods that transmits the motion of the pitman arm of a steering system (Sketch 17, page 219) to the front wheels. The mechanism that causes the hot air to be directed against the windshield when you move a "defroster" lever on the instrument panel is called a linkage, and so is the mechanism that causes the windshield wipers to operate when you move a lever or turn a knob on the instrument panel.

Seal: A doughnut of soft material that prevents leakage of air, oil, water, or refrigerant around a shaft. Thus, the shaft of the water pump must pass through the outer wall of the water pump to be attached to the pulley that drives the pump. Coolant inside the pump is under pressure; it must not be permitted to squirt around the shaft to the outside world; and so a doughnut of appropriate rubbery material is installed to hug the shaft and prevent leakage. Similar seals prevent the leakage of oil around the crankshaft where it goes through the front and rear walls of the crankcase, and around the transmission shafts where they go through the front and rear walls of the transmission case, and around the main shaft of the power-steering pump. There are dozens of other seals in any automobile.

Sending unit: In an automobile, the term refers exclusively to one component of a two-component instrument system. Thus, the gasoline gauge on the instrument panel requires an electrical impulse to operate it, and this impulse is provided by the sending unit located in the gasoline tank; it delivers electrical voltage to the gauge in an amount in proportion to the level of gasoline in the tank. Similarly, the oil-pressure sending unit that is located in an appropriate part of the engine-lubrication system provides electrical voltage (in proportion to the magnitude of the oil pressure) to the gauge or alarm light on the instrument panel. The water-temperature sending unit, located in the water jacket, performs the same function in causing the temperature gauge or alarm light to operate.

Shaft: A cylindrical bar, usually of steel and usually solid (as opposed to hollow), used to support rotating items such as wheels, pulleys, flywheels, etc., or used to transmit power or motion by rotation. There are dozens of shafts of various kinds in an automobile. Sketch 10 (page 191) shows the *drive shaft* (which is usually hollow). The *steering column* shown in Sketch 17 (page 219) is a shaft: it imparts the rotations of the steering wheel to the gearbox. The pivot that the brake pedal swings on (Sketch 14, page 202) is a shaft, because although the motion there is not a complete rotation, it is nevertheless a rotary motion. The water pump and fan (Sketch 7, page 161) operate on the same shaft; and the alternator (Sketch 8, page 170) and the starter (Sketch 1, page 119) are built around main shafts that transmit power from an electrical source to a mechanical load or vice-versa. The crankshaft (Sketch 3, page 128) is perhaps the most important shaft in the automobile: this is the shaft the flywheel rotates on; the U-shaped "crank" sections interrupt the straight line of the shaft, but it both supports rotating items and transmits power by its own rotation.

Solenoid: Generally speaking, a solenoid is a particular kind of coil of electric wire that generates a magnetic field inside the coil when current passes through the wire. In most applications in an automobile, the magnetic field is harnessed to an electrical switch, so that when the current flows through the coil or wire an electromagnet causes the electric switch to be turned on or off. In the most familiar application in an automobile, the *starter solenoid,* the solenoid always operates the heavy-duty switch that supplies current to the starter (see page 120); but in addition to this, in most cars the solenoid also operates a linkage (see page 235) that engages the starter drive gear with the engine flywheel and causes the flywheel to rotate and the engine to start.

Vacuum: A more common word is "suction." The cylinders of a gasoline engine generate a vacuum because within each cylinder the piston, moving downward with the exhaust valve closed (see Sketch 2, page 127), sucks air into the cylinder.

Valve: A valve is a device for controlling the flow of liquid or gas through an opening. The water faucet is a familiar example: by turning the wheel, knob, or lever, you permit or prevent the flow of water and control its rate of flow, and if the valve is faulty, the water will drip instead of stopping when you turn off the valve. There is a similar "screw valve" at the bottom of an automobile radiator so that the coolant can be drained from the cooling system (page 161). There are dozens of other valves in an automobile, of many different types. Most basic is the engine valve, shown in Sketch 21c: a mushroom-shaped object with a beveled edge that rides up and down; when it is tightly closed it seals an opening called a *valve port* and prevents the flow of gasoline/air mixture through the port. Each cylinder of an automobile engine is fitted with two of these valves (see Sketch 2, page 127): one to control the fuel/air mixture into the cylinder, and the other to control the flow of exhaust gas out of the cylinder. Sketch 21b shows the *butterfly,* or *damper,* valve: a flat plate of substantially the same diameter as the pipe it is mounted in; when it is turned crosswise, it blocks the pipe completely; when it is turned longitudinally, it permits almost unrestricted flow through the pipe; and it controls (that is, "throttles") the flow through the pipe when it is in the various positions between the two extremes. The butterfly valve is crucial to the carburetor (Sketch 5, page 144), and it is used to control the flow of air in the heater/defroster/air-

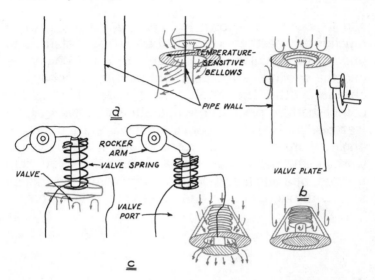

Sketch 21. Three Valves: a) Thermostat Valve, closed (left) and open (right); b) Butterfly Valve (closed); c) Engine Valve, closed (left) and open (right).

conditioner system. The *check valve* is useful throughout an automobile. It is illustrated in Sketch 20a, in the bicycle example. The fuel pump (page 140) depends upon a pair of check valves that permit gasoline to be sucked in from the gasoline tank on an upward stroke of the pump diaphragm, and then to flow out to the carburetor on the downward stroke. The carburetor, the shock absorbers (page 211), and the windshield-washer pump (page 224) all require check valves of one kind or another. The tire valve is still another example of a check valve: when you push the valve stem in by hand it permits air to escape; when you release the stem, a light-weight spring aided by the pressure inside the tire pushes the tire valve closed and prevents further escape of air.

The *thermostat valve* is actuated by the temperature of the fluid it controls. A thermostat valve is shown in Sketch 21a, in both the open and closed positions, and its location is shown in Sketch 7, page 161. The function of the thermostat in the cooling system is to prevent the circulation of coolant when the engine — and the coolant — are cold, but permit the coolant to circulate after the engine warms up. This is accomplished by placing a temperature-sensitive bellows (see Sketch 21a) in the coolant that will warm up as the engine warms up. As the coolant and the bellows get warmer, the bellows expand and push the valve stem upward, opening the valve port and allowing the coolant to flow through, and on through the cooling system.

INDEX